Praise for
When Bad Christians Happen to Good People

"In *When Bad Christians Happen to Good People*, Dave indeed succeeds in making Christians think carefully and in getting us out of our comfort bunkers. I know that Bob would be chuckling with me at Dave's sense of humor as he addresses very tough issues. I recommend it heartily to all who are serious in their commitment to be Jesus to our world."

> —MARTY BRINER, widow of Bob Briner, who authored
> *Roaring Lambs* and *Final Roar*

"Even though I'm not a betting man, I'll bet you've never read a book like this one. Here is a no-holds-barred look at what's right, what's wrong, and what's really weird about the Christian movement in America. At the end of the day, Dave Burchett has a heart for the church, for the gospel, and for people who don't know the Lord. Christians could make a powerful difference in our world. But we ourselves must change. This book points us in the right direction."

> —DR. RAY PRITCHARD, author, conference speaker, and senior pastor
> of Calvary Memorial Church in Oak Park, Illinois

"This book is excellent. Dave Burchett sends a wake up call to all believers that our behavior and our attitudes can have a profound affect on how The Message is received. National research shows that there is a great disparity between how the world views "Christians" and how it views the person of Jesus Christ. *When Bad Christians Happen to Good People* challenges people of faith to live a life that shows the world love, hope, and encouragement."

> —JOHN FROST, noted strategic broadcast consultant

"Dave Burchett is one of the most clever, genuine, and honest people I know. He is a person who walks the talk and speaks from his heart. This book is a must-read for Christians who want to put their faith into action."

—JIM SUNDBERG, major-league ballplayer and author
of *How to Win at Sports Parenting*

"Few contemporary authors can combine excellent research, wit, and the ability to engage the reader in an honest appraisal of his or her spiritual walk. Dave Burchett pulls it off magnificently. *When Bad Christians Happen to Good People* is the best book of its kind I have ever read. Accurate, clear, interesting, relevant. Dave will invade your space. Welcome him."

—REG GRANT, TH.D., professor of pastoral ministries
at Dallas Theological Seminary, director of Media Arts
in Ministry Track, and author

"Dave Burchett strikes out sometimes but happily hits home runs like Sammy Sosa. His comments about the sinner-sensitive church and CSL (Christian as a Second Language), his WJSHTOT question (Would Jesus Spend His Time on This?), and his "Don't Know Much About Theology" song are all terrific."

—MARVIN OLASKY, editor of *World* and senior fellow
of the Acton Institute

"With gentle humor and laserlike insight, Dave Burchett exposes the foibles and inconsistencies we Christians make in our interactions with the world around us. Fortunately, he doesn't leave us exposed and embarrassed. He provides wisdom and a compelling call for authenticity that will help believers be the salt and light Jesus calls us to be."

—DR. STEVE MOORE, Asbury Theological Seminary

When
Bad Christians
Happen to
Good People

When
Bad Christians
Happen to
Good People

WHERE WE HAVE FAILED EACH OTHER
AND HOW TO REVERSE THE DAMAGE

DAVE BURCHETT

WATERBROOK
PRESS

WHEN BAD CHRISTIANS HAPPEN TO GOOD PEOPLE
PUBLISHED BY WATERBROOK PRESS
12265 Oracle Boulevard, Suite 200
Colorado Springs, Colorado 80921
A division of Random House, Inc.

Scripture quotations are taken from the *Holy Bible, New International Version*®. NIV®. Copyright © 1973, 1978, 1984 by International Bible Society. Used by permission of Zondervan Publishing House. All rights reserved.

Italics in quotations reflect the author's added emphasis.

Grateful acknowledgment is made for use of lyrics from *The Rose* by Amanda McBroom. © 1977 Warner-Tamerlane Publishing Corp. and Third Story Music, Inc. All rights administered by Warner-Tamerlane Publishing Corp. All rights reserved. Used by permission. Warner Bros. Publications U.S. Inc., Miami, FL 33014.

ISBN 1-57856-490-5

Library of Congress Cataloging-in-Publication Data
Burchett, Dave.
    When bad Christians happen to good people : where we have failed each other and how to reverse the damage / Dave Burchett.— 1st ed.
        p. cm.
    ISBN 1-57856-490-5
        1. Hypocrisy—Religious aspects—Christianity. 2. Christian life.   I. Title.

BV4627.H8 B87 2001
241—dc21

                                                            2001046634

Printed in the United States of America
2005

10 9 8

On March 27, 1996, I received a fax from my friend Bob Briner. I had written to tell him how much his books (especially *Roaring Lambs*) had meant in my life. Bob had started writing later in his career, and I jokingly told him that I intended to be like him "when I grew up." I told RAB (as his friends called him) how much of an inspiration he had been to me and that I wanted to start writing soon. His return message included the following words:

> Big Dave,
>   You have more writing talent than any of my friends. If you want to write, nothing can stop you.
>   RAB

It was typical Bob, full of encouragement, hope, and perhaps an overestimation of talent! When Bob Briner died in 1999, his exhortation immediately came to mind. I determined then that it was time to "grow up" and begin to follow in my friend's footsteps. This book is dedicated to Bob Briner and his wife, Marty. If God uses this book in any way, it will be just one more jewel in RAB's ministerial crown.

Contents

Part I: Silencing the Lambs
The Indefensible Things We Do to One Another

Part II: Why Won't Those Heathens Listen?
Thoughts on How We Lost Our Audience

Part III: Reality-Based Faith for Survivors

Being Real in an Artificial World

Acknowledgments

Just weeks after deciding to write a book, I had lunch with my friend Ray Pritchard in Chicago. I tentatively showed him my outline and early chapters. He enthusiastically told me that I had "a book in there" and encouraged me to continue. Thanks, Ray, for your support and friendship and for teaching me there is no good writing, just good rewriting.

Thanks to the wonderful folks at WaterBrook Press who were willing to take a chance on this project. Special thanks to my editor, Erin Healy, who has made this a much better book than it would have been without her. I have learned that editors are the unsung heroes in this whole process. Thanks, Erin, for your insight, humor, and unending patience in walking me through each step. You have been a real blessing in my life. Thanks especially for your friendship.

Thanks to my wonderful sons, Matt, Scott, and Brett. It has been a real joy watching each one of you develop into a man of God. All three of you have contributed to this book with your support, love, and encouragement. Thanks for making me look like a far better father than I have probably been. And a special acknowledgment to our golden retriever, Charlie, who has been faithfully at my side for most of this project. If I loved people as much as Charlie does, we would have a perpetual revival in our neighborhood.

Thanks to my wonderful wife and best friend, Joni, who always believes in me, always supports me, and always loves me. You are a gift from God. I love you.

A Brief Disclaimer

When a man who accepts the Christian doctrine lives
unworthily of it, it is much clearer to say he is a bad
Christian than to say he is not a Christian.
—C. S. LEWIS, *Mere Christianity*

I must begin with some words of disclosure. I am a hypocrite. I can be arrogant and selfish. I have been known to stretch, conceal, or slightly massage the truth. I am sometimes inconsiderate and insecure. I struggle with lust and impure thoughts. My ego often rages out of control, and I battle foolish pride. I can be lazy and foolhardy with my time. I get angry, petty, and ill tempered. I am sarcastic and cynical.

I am a Christian.

Does that surprise you? It shouldn't. If there is one theme about our faith that should be communicated, it is that we all fall short of the goal spelled out in Christ's teachings. Author Max Lucado has a wonderful line. He says that God loves you just the way you are, but He refuses to leave you that way. So all of us believers are somewhere on that continuum of where we started

and where God wants us to be. But that realization seems to pene-
trate our thinking only sporadically. In fact, there are those among
us who will call me a counterfeit since I admit to such unflattering
traits. They will write and tell me that if I had their brand of faith,
I would be above any of these sins all of the time. I believe they
would be wrong.

Growing up I always heard a religious person described as
being a "good Christian." When they messed up, I always heard
the deadly, "and he's supposed to be such a good Christian." As a
kid I always wondered why they just didn't say he was a "bad
Christian" like someone was a "bad student" or "bad boy." I guess
they thought that "bad" and "Christian" were mutually exclusive,
but as I've read the Bible I find that isn't always the case. Actually,
most of the "bad" moments of the great women and men of the
Bible are as clearly outlined as the good. King David, described as
a man after God's own heart and the author of some of the most
beautiful praise language in the Psalms, was also an adulterer and
murderer. The apostle Peter went from being a coward who denied
his faith to the rock upon which Christ would build His church.

Like David and Peter, most Christians have both good and bad
traits. I will tell you right up front that I have displayed the latter far
more often than I desire. I have struggled, for example, with the
concept of being judgmental. Matthew 7:1 says, "Do not judge, or
you too will be judged." In many ways that thought is not all that
scary. I know where I stand: "Your honor, before the charges are
read, I would like to plead guilty. I am a sinner."

And yet I remember the time I criticized a Christian friend
about his angry explosion over what seemed to be a trivial issue. I
made some judgmental remarks about his faith. Then I found out

that his mother had died the day before. I felt like a world-class weasel for a couple of days, but then I succumbed to spiritual amnesia and forgot the lesson I'd learned.

Humorist Will Rogers once noted that before a Native American would criticize another man he would walk all the way around that man. He would look carefully to see what the view was from that person's perspective before condemning him. I have to admit I rarely exercise that restraint before donning my judge's robe.

If there are others like me who commit such offenses—and worse—is it any wonder that the unchurched often think we are the biggest single source of phoniness outside of political campaigns?

I must be candid concerning the sad probability that everything negative non-Christians have heard or felt about Christians and the church is partially or even completely true. Many of the unchurched I talk to base their rejection of Christ on a bad experience with a Christian. In reality, that is a lame excuse that disguises the real issues at hand: Who is Jesus Christ and what does that mean?

On the other hand, based on my own informal, unscientific research, I believe a disturbingly high percentage of Christians leave the church and even the faith because of a bad experience with a Christian, a Christian leader, or group of Christians. And that excuse for jumping ship is a smoke screen for the real issues confronting believers: What should a real relationship with Jesus Christ mean and what should our lives look like as a result of that relationship? If we can spend hours, days, and weeks finding the right retirement investment portfolio, dabbling in hobbies, or developing our bowling form, then we should be able to squeeze out a little time when we get up in the morning to understand Christ's claims and what they mean—regardless of our experiences with other Christians.

Even though we must learn to look past the actions of some Christians and focus on Christ, it is still impossible to justify the indefensible things we Christians do to one another.

I have heard an amazing array of stories from Christians who have been victims of emotional drive-by shootings in the church. Most of us Christians have been wounded by "friendly fire" somewhere along our journey. Whether that fire is intentional or not, the scars are still real.

This book is written for the person who has been hurt by a judgmental or unfriendly church. For the woman who has been sexually or emotionally abused by a Christian man. For the guy ripped off by a businessman brandishing a Christian symbol on his sign or business cards. For the teenage girl rejected by the church for an out-of-wedlock pregnancy. For the person made to feel unwelcome because of color or position in life. For the man or woman driven away because of appearance or dress. For the people who felt uncomfortable in the place where they should feel most welcome. This book is for everyone who has been disgusted by the hypocritical arrogance of a church congregation or its leadership.

This book is also for Christians who inflicted the wounds. Would it surprise you to learn that there is probably a significant overlap between these two audiences? It is human nature to respond in kind. If I am judged or rejected, my first reaction is to judge and reject.

At the bottom line, this book is for Christians living in frustration because of other Christians. It is for those who are frustrated by their own spiritual shortcomings but especially the shortcomings of others. And it is for those who have divorced (or at least separated themselves from) the church because of that frustration. I have talked to numerous believers who are so obsessed about the weaknesses of others that they can't see anything else. And so this book is for those who have been frustrated by others for so many years that they have lost touch with their own relationship with Christ.

Now, if we can't get our own Christian relationships in order, how can we expect to do better with unbelievers? Those of us who follow Christ in this culture will never achieve all that He desires for us until we are willing to open every nook and cranny of our own behavioral house for remodeling and cleaning. Only then will we begin to live the kind of lives that others will find intriguing and distinctive.

Perhaps you are so spiritually mature that you can't relate to any of this. At any rate I have always said my ministry was to make other Christians feel superior. I am still trying to comprehend what the grace of God means after over thirty-plus years of sprinting, stumbling, falling, crawling, back-pedaling, jogging, and limping through my Christian experience.

In this book we will look at some steps to locate the nearly extinct species known as personal responsibility. We will examine ways to not worry about those things over which we have no control (other people and circumstances) and look at how to take charge of the things we can control (how Jesus impacts our lives). Baseball player Mickey Rivers wasn't much of a theologian (trust me on this one), but he did offer some pretty good advice: "Don't worry about things that you have no control over because you have no control over them. Don't worry about things that you have control over because you have control over them." If you need a more biblical basis than Mickey Rivers, try Deuteronomy 29:29: "The secret things belong to the LORD our God, but the things revealed belong to us and to our children forever." In other words, there are some things you have no control over. So do something about those things revealed to us.

In this book we will also spend time reevaluating the things we are doing as a church and why we are doing them. The principle "We have always done it this way" should be banned from every sanctuary and replaced with the prayerful inquiry, "Is this still the best way to do this?" A church that is not relevant will not change lives, and I must note here that being relevant does not necessarily mean being culturally hip. It simply means being able and willing to address the big questions and concerns all of us have. Why am I here? Where do I find significance? Can marriage and family still work even in this culture? What should I do with my life? What happens when I die? Why is there pain and suffering if God is really watching and involved? The questions go on, and they don't get easier. Are we willing to counter doubt and weakness with patience and encouragement?

At the same time we must also reevaluate the church strategies and programs that we have changed and why we have changed them. Recently my wife, Joni, and I decided our home needed a face-lift. Our fifteen-year-old carpet was on life support. So we decided to change the carpet and do some other updating. But we didn't tear up the foundation to replace the carpet. We changed what needed to be changed and kept the rest. Yet I fear that many churches have torn out pretty solid foundations just to keep up with the latest trends. Was the change merely for the sake of change? Did we throw out the baby Jesus with the baptismal water? Have we gotten caught up in the trend of seeking a cozy relationship with God and lost sight of His majesty? In this book we will seek to balance old and new.

If we truly want to find that balance, we must be willing to go through self-examination even if it hurts and forces us out of our little comfort bunkers. We must be willing to be brutally honest with ourselves. During a recent presidential campaign, the slogan was "It's the economy, stupid." The campaign did not want to lose the focus of what they needed to communicate to win. I really don't mean to offend anyone (yet), but for Christians, "It's the gospel, stupid." Nothing else should take precedent over that priority. In our dealings with one another and in our dealings with our culture, we should have that commission as our rudder. We may do lots of other things to accomplish that goal, but we must always keep the focus of the gospel of Christ.

My hope is that this book will be thought provoking for Christians who realize that things must change within our church community if we hope to communicate more effectively the life-changing message of the gospel. We will have to model Christ more consistently. We will have to give up those smoke-screen issues that are great for debating but just don't amount to a hill of beans for eternity. We will have to be more thoughtful in discerning the difference, and I hope to provoke your thoughts in that area.

This book is the result of a very personal journey. After thirty-one years of roller-coaster faith, I decided to examine nearly every aspect of my spiritual house. Some components needed just a little cleaning and polishing. Some had to be discarded. Some parts of my faith required a major remodeling that is far from over. These writings reflect some of that journey.

Now, as I ponder the title of this book, I realize that there is a very fine line between being thought provoking and being a jerk. Perhaps you think I've already crossed it. I admit, at times I will be harsh and confrontational. But I have no desire to send you on lengthy guilt trips. Travel agencies for guilt trips would seem to be a saturated market anyway. Even so, I intend to be honest with myself and with you. One of the interesting things that has happened as I have been writing this book is seeing how God has turned my words back on me. In many ways it has been like watching a Bugs Bunny cartoon. I am Elmer Fudd loading up my shotgun blast of criticism. Then God bends the gun barrel around, and I am blasted with my own buckshot.

So I hope we can have a laugh or two and open our minds to what "Christian" should mean when we claim the title. Let's get real for a little while. Let's be honest about our Christian appearance, warts and all. Let's be introspective without being obsessive. Let's look at what we have wrought with a balance of candor and humor since I have found that a little of both (along with a lot of humility and repentance) are necessary for change. Let's ask God to show us our weaknesses.

Who the heck am I to ask these hard questions and issue such personal challenges? I'm just a regular guy who wants to see people experience the freedom and joy that come only (in my experience) through a real relationship with Jesus Christ. I'm a guy who's trying to live Christianity without the smoke screens of the unimportant and phony excuses that lead to paralysis. A person looking to live my faith without doing damage to those I encounter in the daily chaos. I want to be a man who does no harm to the wonderful name of Jesus or to my brothers and sisters in Christ. That is a lofty target, and it is one I have already missed. I will no doubt miss it again and again. But it is a target that I believe you and I can hit with greater frequency. And it is a target that we must aim for every single day. I possess neither a theological doctorate nor a seminary degree. But reality is that perspective can be gained in many ways. If I am swimming in the ocean and I spot a shark, I can assure you that I won't need a marine biology degree to get my posterior out of the water.

I only ask that you understand that my goal is to make you think, to challenge you to reexamine. I will probably offend you along the way. (That's okay. You have a contractual obligation to forgive me anyway.) Just remember in the Old Testament book of Numbers 22:28, you will find this statement:

"Then the LORD opened the donkey's mouth..."

Hey, it can happen!

Part I

Silencing the Lambs

The Indefensible Things We Do to One Another

Chapter 1

The Unfriendliest Club in Town?

*The greatest single cause of atheism in the world today is
Christians who acknowledge Jesus with their lips then
walk out the door and deny him by their lifestyle. That is
what an unbelieving world simply finds unbelievable.*

—BRENNAN MANNING

A uthor Flannery O'Connor once noted that "sometimes you
have to suffer as much *from* the church as you do *for* it."
Perhaps the most painful experience of my marriage came courtesy
of the church.

My wife, Joni, gave birth to our daughter in 1985. But our
happiness dissolved into grief when we learned Katie had a terminal neural tube birth defect called anencephaly, which had pre-
vented her brain from developing. She basically had just the brain
stem. Katie was not expected to live more than a few hours or

days. The doctor in the delivery room described Katie's situation in physicianspeak that I will never forget. "Her condition is not compatible with life," he said.

Our shock and grief were immediate because Katie obviously had no chance for a normal life. There would be no cure, no hope for even modest improvement. I went through the painful process of calling family and friends and telling our two sons about their sister.

But Kathryn Alice Burchett confounded the doctors and lived. She was never able to open her eyes. She couldn't smile. Katie lacked the ability to regulate her body temperature so her room temperature had to be monitored. Part of Katie's deformity was an opening with exposed tissue at the back of her skull that had to be covered and dressed regularly. Joni loved and cared for Katie in a way I will always respect and never forget. She insisted that Katie come home with us. I worried about the effect that caring for Katie at home might have on the boys. Truthfully, I was probably more concerned about the effect bringing her home would have on me. But Joni would not have it any other way, and when she sets her mind she is scrappy. So I showed my spiritual wisdom by agreeing with her.

Katie found her place in our family's routines. She could drink from a bottle. Katie responded to her mother's touch and even grew a little. We took her on a camping trip with us, and she was a regular at the boy's ball games and events.

Sometimes people would make hurtful or mean remarks. A kid at school taunted our oldest son because his sister didn't have a brain. (That was something that the classmate had no doubt heard at home, and it reminds me that we should always be cautious about what we say in front of our children.) Once, when we wanted a family photo, we dressed up the troops and went to the photography studio of a major national chain. The photographer insisted that Katie needed to open her eyes. We explained patiently (for a while) that she physically could not open her eyes. He informed us that we couldn't get our picture taken because their lab would not develop a picture if any person in the group didn't have their eyes open. Katie totally upset their system, and they would not be flexible. We finally left without the photos and ended up going to a private photographer. Still, all things considered, our life with Katie went about as well as it could.

Then the church entered in.

One Sunday morning before church, a friend called to tell us that Katie would no longer be welcome in the nursery. The moms had met and decided (without any input from us) that Katie might die in their care and traumatize some volunteer worker. They worried that the opening at the back of Katie's skull could generate a staph infection. Actually, the nursery workers did not have to deal with infection; the opening was covered with a sterile dressing and a bonnet, and it required no special attention during the brief time she was in the nursery each Sunday. Besides, Katie did not interact with the other babies. Clearly, a little caution would have eliminated any possible risk. And we knew she was going to die. No one would have been to blame. Since we were in a church of only 150 people, I think they could have found us fairly quickly if necessary. Given the opportunity, we might have been able to put the workers' fears to rest. But the decision had already been made. Katie was no longer welcome, and our church had done what I would not have thought possible: They made our pain worse.

Joni was devastated, more hurt than I have ever seen her before or since. I am sure our friends didn't intend to wound as they did, but the hurt lingered for years. And the pain was multiplied by the method. We had no warning that there were concerns. We received no invitation to address those concerns. Instead, a secret meeting was followed by a phone call to tell us what had already been decided. And I'm not the only one with this kind of story.

I know a pastor in the Midwest who suffered the tragic loss of his wife to leukemia. Within a matter of weeks, the board asked him to resign because they did not want to be led by an unmarried pastor! This grieving man had to change denominations in order to continue his ministry. It is a miracle and tribute to God's grace that he kept going at all.

In my hometown of Chillicothe, Ohio, an acquaintance finally decided it was time to get his family into a local church. He loaded up the crew and visited one nearby. The church immediately showed a tremendous and heartfelt concern for his...grooming issues. You see, Roy had the audacity to show up in God's house with a full beard, not unlike Jesus' in the picture hanging in the foyer. A church leader met Roy on the way out.

"So are you going to start worshiping with us?" he asked.

"Why yes," Roy replied. "We want to start coming to church."

The church leader looked at him and said, "Well, I hope you will have shaved by next Sunday." That was over twenty years ago. Roy has still not found a regular church home.

HYPOCRITES OR HEALERS?

The word *hypocrite* comes from the Greek word *hyprokrites,* meaning one who plays a part, an actor. Probably no word is more destructively used in describing Christians than *hypocrite.* André Gide once defined a true hypocrite (an oxymoron?) as the "one who ceases to perceive his deception, the one who lies with sincerity."

Inevitably, my first and natural reaction upon hearing the word is to think of people I consider guilty of hypocrisy. When the Reverend Jesse Jackson revealed his relationship with a mistress, I pulled out my hypocrite hammer to smite him. My first reaction should be to ask God to search me and see if a similar lack of discernment lives in my own heart. Somehow, that request has not yet become automatic.

One of Christ's severest rebukes concerned the hypocrisy of the Pharisees (Matthew 6). These religious leaders liked to be seen and heard when praying, recognized when giving, and pitied when fasting. Had the Jerusalem Broadcasting Network been on the air, you just know that some slick-haired Pharisees would have hosted the prime-time programs.

Today the church condemns those who drink and smoke and live immoral lives while we churchgoers engage in gluttony and gossip and selfishness and bigotry. The unchurched stand by in amazed, bemused, cynical, or angry observance of our hypocrisy. And they lose respect for our message.

As a young man, I sat through many sermons about devil alcohol and demon tobacco followed by a church potluck where apparently the demon of calories was a welcome guest. It seems to me that morbid obesity is also a desecration of the temple (our body). Is that not also wrong? Overweight churchgoers often explain their extra pounds by citing low metabolism or thyroid disorders. I acknowledge that, for many, there is a legitimate medical reason why weight gain is a constant struggle. But shouldn't we also keep open at least the *possibility* that someone's addiction to nicotine might be similarly genetically predisposed? Or that someone with a weakness for alcohol or pills could possibly be related to a brain chemistry imbalance that exacerbates that problem?

Before you dash off to write a nasty letter of condemnation for my views (you will have many more opportunities; I suggest you keep a running tab and send a comprehensive diatribe later), let me say that I believe with all of my being in the life-changing power of God. I know He can empower an alcoholic to become and stay dry. I have witnessed that fact. I believe God can give a smoker the strength to snuff out that last cigarette. I am convinced God can enable a person to flush pills and drugs down the drain once and for all. But isn't there an uncomfortable flip side to that faith? Shouldn't we also acknowledge that God can give us the power to walk away from the buffet table? That He can give me the strength to bridle my tongue when I become privy to gossip that would hurt another person? Should I not recognize that God can enable me to keep driving that unsexy old car or keep watching that small screen television with no picture-in-picture in order to free up my resources to help someone in need of life's *actual* necessities?

I marvel at the example of Christ and His approach to sinners. Obviously He could not possibly have condoned the lifestyles and actions of many who surrounded Him. Yet He seemed drawn to the spiritually needy—and they to Him. Prostitutes, lepers, and tax collectors all felt the need to hear what Jesus had to say. (Note to my IRS friends: In that culture tax collectors were turncoats who unfairly extorted their own people for personal gain. Nothing at all like the honorable members of our fine government tax organization evaluating my home-office deductions on this year's tax return.)

It seems that the people most uncomfortable around Jesus were the religious, the churchgoers as it were. Those who are most ill need the physician's time, and Jesus gravitated to the ER cases. I have friends who are physicians, and probably no patient annoys them more than a hypochondriac. These unfortunate people drain the resources and time of medical personnel, resources, and time that could be far better used healing the truly sick. It seems to me that Jesus dealt with the hypochondriacs of His day (the Pharisees and religious people) with that same attitude. Jesus had little patience with those who failed to recognize their true spiritual symptoms. But He was always willing to see the spiritually ill.

The church should be in the business of addressing spiritual illness. When you are deathly ill, you don't start thinking of going to the health club: "Well, this will be a good time to get in shape. I feel horrible, and I think I'm going to die." Yet many churches have somehow communicated that only the spiritually healthy are truly welcome at church. Many people think their lives are too far gone to be accepted at church, when in fact that brokenness just about makes them ready to receive God's amazing grace. But too many feel that going to church would make them too uncomfortable or heighten their guilt. They sense they would be judged and treated with condescension.

Yes, some of these feelings are self-inflicted wounds. But more are not. We must examine the possibility that we are doing things that make hurting people stay away from the church. Do you ever think your health is too messed up to go to the hospital? Assuming you have insurance, does a hospital ever communicate that you are just a little too sick to come in? "We don't like the look of your illness. Find another place to go." When did the church step away from its responsibility of healing emotional pain and meeting physical, emotional, and spiritual needs? Steve Martin used to say, "Comedy isn't pretty." Sometimes ministry isn't either. Sometimes it won't be neat or polished or slick. Sometimes it requires us to pay a price.

Most of us don't much like to be around the truly spiritually ill. It tends to make us uncomfortable. Treating the spiritually ill is draining, and it comes with no guarantees for success. We would rather hire someone to clean up the mess and report back to us at a praise service.

Yet how can we preach Christ's love and not care about the AIDS epidemic? So what if it doesn't "touch" us or if we find its primary means of transmission unsettling? How can we talk about God's grace but ignore other people's physical needs and bow to the idols of success and money and power? How can we talk about the importance of giving, and then spend money on things we don't need, often to curry the approval of people we don't really care about? How can we minister to others when we don't first meet the spiritual needs of our own families? How can we win the respect of the world when we cruise around in luxury sports cars and turn our faces away from homeless people?

Do we think that if we ignore the problems perhaps God will not hold us accountable?

Our family has a wonderful golden retriever named Charlie. He is a connoisseur of used Kleenex and paper towels. Charlie knows I disapprove of him running off with tissues, so each time he nabs one, he dashes to the family room and sticks his head and front quarters under a Queen Anne chair. Charlie doesn't realize that 75 percent of his body is sticking out and his tail is wagging wildly. He thinks he is safe from retribution because his face is hidden. It is a ridiculous and humorous scene.

Is it any less ridiculous to think that we Christians can avoid our responsibilities as Christ's representatives and operatives on this planet? Are we Christians any smarter than Charlie when we avert our gaze from the needs of others and convince ourselves that God won't notice? Somehow I don't think God smiles and says, "Oh, that Dave, he was just too busy to notice his friend was in pain. But that's okay. " No. Instead, my selfishness sticks out just as noticeably as Charlie's rear end. (There is a certain symmetry in that analogy.)

COUNTRY CLUB CHRISTIAN

I was raised in a very strict church where rules and regulations smothered the concept of grace by their sheer weight. No jewelry for women. No mixed bathing. (That one was a wild fantasy for my adolescent hormones until I realized they meant swimming.) No musical instruments other than a piano or organ in the church. I never did find the biblical basis for that one.

"And thou shalt have no stringed instruments or percussive idols."

No long hair for men. No short hair for women. No shorts. No cussing. No makeup. No pants for women. No card playing. No movies. No dancing. No smoking. No drinking. I actually sat through a sermon where the preacher spent sixty minutes trying to explain that the wine of the New Testament was actually grape juice. So Jesus turned the water into Welch's? What a wedding feast that must have been with great food and a fine vintage grape juice.

"It's a lovely little vintage…stomped just this morning."

On and on the list went. If any activity involved an ounce of pleasure, you could be pretty sure the answer was no. No television. People in our church used to put a sheet over the television when the preacher made a house call. As if the good reverend wouldn't know that a "Devil's Box" stood under that cover. Obviously God wouldn't know either. I mean, how could the Creator of the universe *possibly* know that the box-shaped object under the big sheet was a television?

The list of no's went on and on. The effect was predictable: We experienced no joy, no peace, no assurance of God's forgiveness—and no interest from anyone outside our miserable little circle. I suggested renaming our sullen little group the First Church of Misery Loves Company but We Probably Won't Love You.

Some of the things allowed in this church were really more repulsive than the things banned. Things like racism and bigotry. There was not a stated policy, but you would have never seen a "colored" (our loving and enlightened term for African-Americans) in our church. It was just understood. They had "their" churches, and I guess we thought it was okay for "them" to worship "our" God if "they" had the decency to be discreet about it. Actually only the more spiritual in our body called African-Americans "coloreds." For the less enlightened it was "darkies" or worse. Members of our church also railed against Jews. I have heard from the pulpit how the Jews were ruining our country, while the fact that the Savior happened to be one was ignored. And don't even begin to mention "queers" or "sodomites," as we so colorfully called the gay population.

No wonder so many people feel so alienated from the church. I often feel alienated—and I'm a member of this club!

But Jesus' church is not a highbrow country club. The church should exclude no one. The church should welcome those unwelcome anywhere else. Anyone can attend. And yet most churches are not a place where people feel comfortable if they are living a life that is not moral. In fact, the church is often a place where most people don't feel comfortable if they're just living life.

Apart from God's grace and the maturity to see each human being as His creation, we are prone to reject those who are different from us. Have you ever wished that certain people wouldn't speak or be so prominent in your congregation? You would be more comfortable bringing unchurched friends if those slightly embarrassing brothers and sisters weren't there, or at least were invisible. My family reunion would look much better (trust me) if it were by invitation only. But when you include the entire family, you get a few embarrassments. And your family is no doubt the same. So it is with my church family. That is a simple fact, given what we have to work with: sinners.

We need to trust God with those who are a little embarrassing to those of us who are not. (How amazing that our prideful minds can even think like that.) We might even take the bold step of befriending them. Believers who hang around with a homogeneous group of carbon-copy Christians limit their own growth. But more on that in the next chapter.

THE SINNER-SENSITIVE CHURCH

I recall dating a girl long before I met my beloved Joni. (This book-writing stuff is dangerous.) I asked her to go to church with me. She was not a Christian and did not know the official rules. As you might have gathered, our church published them in a multivolume set. She arrived at church wearing a strapless dress that the congregation found scandalous. In her mind she was simply wearing her best dress to church; she had no idea she was doing anything wrong. Actually, she wasn't doing anything wrong, but you get the point. From the moment we walked in, the two of us felt the saints' reproachful laser-beam stares of righteousness drilling into us. Instead of asking God to make her heart receptive to His Word, I spent the service worrying about what this pea-brained congregation thought of me. I must be honest and report that a handful of gracious people in the body welcomed us, but most folks were just busy being appalled.

This would not happen in the sinner-sensitive church.

The sinner-sensitive church (SSC) is my proposal for a new church movement toward making everyone feel welcomed and loved. The SSC would model nonjudgmental attitudes. Issues like having tattoos, body piercings, weird hair, or ugly shoes would not necessarily denote demon possession. The SSC would pledge not to gossip because we would realize that it is only by the grace of God that we are not the current targets. The sinner-sensitive church would value every spiritual, physical, and financial gift, no matter how big or small. This church would appreciate but not elevate the person who built the new wing with the large financial endowment. The SSC would make it a practice to reach out, touch, and care for one another sacrificially because we know that we all fall down in life and in our Christian walk. At the SSC we would have executives holding hands in prayer with laborers and not thinking twice about it. Blacks and whites and Hispanics and others would break bread together because we are all sinners in the eyes of a color-blind God.

The sinner-sensitive church would give freely out of profound gratitude to a God who somehow saw fit to give us an undeserved chance. The sinner-sensitive church would practice the prodigal son ministry, running to welcome those returning from mistakes and bad decisions and sin. Our members would get involved in other people's lives. We would hold our brothers and sisters accountable to godly standards. Marriage would be cherished. Families would have a community of support during problems and trials. The congregation of the SSC would not be so self-centered that we would demand the undivided attention of the pastor at every little crisis. Other believers would help meet many of those needs that we now prefer to leave to the "professional Christians" on staff. The people of this church would come with hearts ready to be fed but also realizing that God has provided resources beyond any available in history to meet our spiritual hunger. And should we walk out the church doors still needy, we would know we can draw from the marvelous resources of Christian books, music, radio, video, tapes, Internet, and studies to meet our needs. Any one of us could be filled to overflowing if that were our desire.

The sinner-sensitive church would also delight in the company of other spiritual travelers and make it a priority that no one ever felt alone. We would make each other feel valuable but, on occasion, a little uncomfortable. Being comfortable in church is not the primary goal. I am not always comfortable at the dentist's office. I often arrive in pain because I have neglected to do what I should have done. The staff always makes me feel welcome and even cared for. Then the dentist confronts me with the truth: "You have let this go too long, and I must hurt you (a little) in order to heal you. You will have to pay a financial price and spend time recovering before you are completely well." Those are the facts of my dental hygiene sin. The sinner-sensitive church would not back off the truth either. Decay in the enamel or soul must be addressed. We will tell one another the truth and explain that the process might be a little painful. We would participate in ongoing preventative maintenance and help one another deal with problems as soon as possible, before they become even more painful and expensive to fix.

The SSC would worship with enthusiasm, whether singing hymns or praise choruses, because God is worthy of that praise. The sinner-sensitive fellowship would have a sense of profound reverence because we have received God's grace, the most amazing gift ever offered. The sinner-sensitive church would be so excited about this grace that the incredible news of the gospel would be as much a part of who we are as our jobs and our families.

Sinner sensitive was the ministry style of our Lord. He was always available to people who realized their need. Merely being a seeker did not necessarily merit His time. The wealthy young man came to Jesus seeking what he lacked to receive eternal life (Matthew 19:16-22). However, the jarring truth of Christ's answer to sell his possessions and give to the poor revealed to him that he was not ready to follow Christ. But when sinners came with a humble confession of need and a willingness to obey God, Jesus never turned them away. The church of Acts was sinner-sensitive and functioned much in the way I have described above. (I'm not sure about the praise choruses though.)

Frankly, sometimes we try a little too hard to "attract" the unchurched. A church that functioned like the one described above would be such a societal miracle that you couldn't keep people away if you barred the doors. And while the majority of my idealism has been beaten out of me, I still believe that such a church will be possible when we finally reach the point of actually wanting it. That will not come until we decide we are willing to pay the price for such a church. The harsh reality is that most of us are afraid to commit to this radical type of fellowship because we aren't sure what it would require of us. My own natural reaction is "Praise the Lord but keep the Lexus!" I'll hazard a guess that you are the same. When the young rich man in Matthew heard Jesus' words to him, "he went away sad, because he had great wealth."

GOVERNED BY GRACE

Phillip Yancey has written a wonderful book about grace entitled *What's So Amazing About Grace?* that I would put on anyone's must-read list. One of his most compelling illustrations comes from an alcoholic friend who attends Alcoholics Anonymous meetings. His friend says, "When I'm late to church, people turn around and stare at me with frowns of disapproval. I get the clear message that I'm not as responsible as they are. When I'm late to AA, the meeting comes to a halt, and everyone jumps up to hug and welcome me. They realize that my lateness may be a sign that I almost didn't make it."

Wouldn't you love to see this scenario play out at a local church: I walk in as a visitor and stride to the front of the sanctuary during the multimedia drama presentation about accepting others' differences. I turn to the congregation and announce, "Hi! My name is Dave. And I'm a sinner."

"Hi, Dave!" the congregation responds. "We love you and we are here to help."

More likely an associate pastor would gently take me by the arm and try to lead me quietly away while a deacon called the straitjacket express. Today's successful twelve-step support groups have become what the body of Christ could and, in fact, should have become. And while the roots of Alcoholics Anonymous are firmly planted in Christian grace, why did it even have to be developed? Shouldn't the church be the place to which such hurting men and women would instinctively be drawn to receive the help they need?

Even a quick study of the life of Christ would reveal that any of us could have quite comfortably walked into His "twelve guy" program and announced our status as sinners. In fact, that little confession would have moved us right to the head of the class and could very well have made us teacher's pet. So why has the local church repelled so many of those who have the very needs we are equipped, through Christ, to address? I realize that it is not entirely the fault of the church that the spiritually ill stay away. But it seems to me that we had better examine what part of the problem is our responsibility.

When I was a kid, the spread of tuberculosis was a big concern. Those with the disease were isolated in a hospital-like dormitory with the scary name "sanatorium." Whenever I'd pass the sanatorium in our town, I would look fearfully at the building. I knew the people inside had something I did not want to come in contact with under any circumstances. And I have a sick feeling in the pit of my stomach today that many people drive by their local church with that same fear and resolve to avoid contact with us at all costs.

But the church should be the most level playing field on earth. After all, in Jesus' eyes, the soul of the Fortune 500 CEO is no more valuable than the soul of the crackhead down the alley. That sort of thinking is uncomfortable and even scandalous for most of us because it contradicts our culture's values. We honor looks, money, power, and fame. Jesus cared about none of those. In Luke 16:14 the gospel writer talked about "the Pharisees, who loved money, [and] heard all this [Jesus talking about the parable of the shrewd manager] and were sneering at Jesus [a phrase that I hope to never see next to my name]." He said to them, "You are the ones who justify yourselves in the eyes of men, but God knows your hearts. What is *highly valued among men is detestable in God's sight*" (verse 15). I am constantly amazed that the words of Jesus apply just as accurately to the stories that appear in *USA Today* as they did to stories in the *Galilee Gazette* two thousand years ago.

Through the years I have thought about what would have happened if Jesus Himself had walked into the nursery where our daughter, Katie, was unwelcome. I am convinced of several things based on my study of His life. He likely would have been drawn straight to her. He might have chosen to heal her. He probably would have shed a tear because the suffering of children always touched His heart. And I am absolutely sure of one thing: He would not have rejected her. I believe that He would have comforted Joni and me with the reassurance that her affliction was not the result of our sin.

The popular saying What Would Jesus Do? can be a bit trite, but on the other hand it can pose a great spiritual question. Our church never asked that question concerning little Katie Burchett. Joni and I left that church that day for good.

Christians, like physicians, should vow to do no harm. But forgive us, Lord.

Because we do.

Note: In honor of the great Paul Harvey, later I will tell you the "rest of the story" about little Katie.

Chapter 2

The Schism Trail

A man was shipwrecked on a remote island for twenty years.
After nearly giving up hope, he finally spotted a ship on the
horizon. He set off flares, attracted the attention of the sailors,
and they rescued him from the island. As they were leaving the
captain noticed three structures on the island. Impressed, the
captain inquired about the buildings.

"The one on the left is my house," the man noted. "And the
one on the right is my church."

"Then what is the building in the middle?" the captain asked.

"That one?" the man sniffed. "That's the church I used to go to!"

        —CHRISTIAN HUMOR WEB

The Chisholm Trail begins in my adopted home state of Texas. Millions of cattle were once driven north along that trail to Kansas. Those unfortunate cattle were shipped by rail to the eastern United States and slaughtered. The Schism Trail is also located in my home state. In fact, this trail of church division can be found in virtually every Christian church and organization in the world. Here millions of believers and nonbelievers are driven to spiritual distraction by bickering over issues that are often minor or, at best, secondary concerns. Regarding the slaughter part, I'll let you make your own observations.

Whenever we Christians come to a fork in the Schism Trail, we seem incapable of peacefully arriving at a consensus. Nope. We have ourselves a little saints' shootout right then and there. Then the "victors" leave the victims behind and stagger down their chosen path.

I have attended eight churches over the course of my life. Six of those have experienced some degree of schism or split while I was attending. I was fortunate not to be embroiled in the middle of any of the divisions. Yet even as a disheartened observer I was affected.

WE'RE A MOTLEY CREW

The Schism Trail eventually winds its way through more churches than not. Caron de Beaumarchais observed, "It is not necessary to understand things in order to argue about them." We prove his point Sunday after Sunday. It is a symptom of our dysfunction. The church is dysfunctional because it can't be anything else. Seriously. Just look at who attends. The church is comprised of people at all levels of spiritual understanding, commitment, and maturity. The church could appear as a guest on *Montel, Jenny Jones,* or sometimes even *Springer.* In the first chapter I examined the damage that is caused when the church excludes certain people from its family. The paradox of Christ's church is that bringing in everyone also creates problems.

Imagine an athletic team attempting to operate as a church

must. You start with a couple of All-Americans and a few other pretty good players. But you also have several who just started playing and don't even know the rules or terminology of the game. Add some dreadfully out-of-shape, middle-aged players who have been around for years, who never work out or train, but who expect to get playing time nonetheless. You have a few who just don't care anymore and don't want to practice, learn the plays, or listen to the coach. But you can't cut them from the team or even bench them without causing big problems. There are some who try hard but are too weak or injury prone to be effective. A few regularly miss games and practices without notice and then reappear expecting to play and even start. Toss in some...um..."mature" players who remember the way the game was played back when it was good. You also have some players who think the coach and his assistants are total idiots. Some passionately believe that the offensive game plan is totally wrong and that all the other players need to change to comply with their personal team philosophy...now! And then you have some who try to run their own plays when they go in the game. Many of the players meet regularly at Denny's immediately after each game to disparage the coach and staff after saying grace over a Grand Slam breakfast.

How do you think this team would perform? If they ever won a game, it would be a miracle. Yet we have a church team with those same dynamics, and we seem surprised by its dysfunction. Sure, we could fix the church just like you would go about fixing the football team. Hold spiritual tryouts for all Christians before you let them join the church. Cut most of the rookie Christians or send them to another church to get experience. Waive all the Christians with bad attitudes or a poor work ethic. Fine those

Christians who are late to meetings. Make the deacons run laps when they miss a row while passing the offering basket. Assign fifty push-ups to the pastor if the sermon goes into overtime. (I rather like that one.) With a little discipline you could shape up the church and make it look impressive on the surface, but it would cease to be the church of the New Testament.

I have reached the conclusion that lack of unity may be the single biggest problem in the universal church and, of course, in our individual fellowships. When a major league baseball team starts to lose games regularly, it is said to have "bad clubhouse chemistry." That's a fancy way of saying, "This team doesn't get along, and the players don't work well together." How sad that "congregational chemistry" has the same effect on winning...only our losses are eternal.

I know of a church that has quadrupled in size in the past two years. The church is growing, and lives are changing. But the Schism Trail has wound its way into the church. One of the long-time members is convinced that the church is sliding straight to hell because...women are wearing slacks to church. I can't even laugh anymore. When you see 75 percent more people seeking what you ostensibly believe in with all of your being, how can your primary concern be clothing? Similar examples are far more common than I care to think about. We talk about multiplication of our ministry, but we seem to only really understand division. If a house divided cannot stand, it will have an even harder time attracting enthusiastic crowds.

If Christians are onto something that is life changing, if we possess a relationship worth dying for, if we believe in something enough to change our very worldview in order to embrace it, then why are we arguing about things like whether women can teach in the church? In a world that is clearly on a moral slippery slope, why are we debating whether seeker-sensitive churches are more effective than traditional ones? Here are the kinds of questions floating around many congregations today: Is contemporary worship required to reach the boomer generation? Is the average person's attention span too short for a traditional sermon? Should we project the Scripture on the screens so that people without Bibles won't feel uncomfortable? Should we have a worship band? Praise team? Choir? Video in the presentation? PowerPoint graphics? Dramas to illustrate key points?

Obviously any church needs to have a prayerfully designed strategy regarding its approach to ministry. But I would also suggest that we easily become unbalanced—and prone to division—when we argue method over message. Over the course of my life I have seen church strategies come and go. Some of the churches I've attended have jumped on the bandwagon of new ideas. Some very comfortably stayed with the format and hymnals they brought with them on the Mayflower. My point is simply this: There are a lot of styles and ways of coming together in fellowship to worship Christ. (I've elaborated on my personal vision in chapter 1.) Yet, there is no right way or wrong way to come to Christ in worship except as it pertains to the heart attitude you bring through the door with you.

FEEDING FRENZY

I recently visited the National Aquarium in New Orleans. The aquarium featured a large display tank filled with piranha. I watched with fascination as the deadly fish swam quietly and peacefully. There was little indication that they could devour an unfortunate victim in minutes. I read the information posted about that species of piranha. They are peaceful when they are fed and when normal food sources are available. But when the water gets a little low, they begin to feel crowded and threatened. Add hunger to the equation and their entire personality changes. The piranhas get angry, aggressive, and prone to feeding frenzies. They begin to attack everything in the water, including one another.

Christians can become emotional piranhas. When we are well fed and happy, we swim peacefully around and are relaxing to watch. When Christians start a feeding frenzy, it can often be traced to a type of hunger as well. Spiritual hunger attacks can sometimes be caused by a lack of biblical fish food. But often the feeding frenzy begins just because the water is getting too crowded and we are too lazy (or stubborn) to find food ourselves. Perhaps there are too many new species in the tank, and the school just isn't the same anymore. In any case, it gets ugly when the piranhas in the pews aren't happy anymore. For this species of Christian, being happy is best defined as "getting my way." So the frenzy begins. It doesn't matter whether you are a pastor, elder, youth pastor, worship leader, or mere fellow worshiper; no one is safe.

It is my observation that even just one little grumpy piranha can stir up a whole school of frenzied attackers. In the wild, piranhas try to isolate their prey before attacking it. Generally the tail region is the first area to be attacked. Since that is just too easy, you can draw your own parallels to the Christian analogy. I am convinced that if you could just spear the lead piranha, most church schisms would be dead in the water (sorry). But Scripture and state laws being what they are, that approach is unacceptable. Seriously, I have witnessed many Christians get into an emotional feeding frenzy and leave dear, long-term church relationships. I am convinced that many of these people would never have considered such a dramatic move of their own volition. They left in large part because of the emotions stirred up by the school. In the frenzy, leaving seems like the only thing to do. It is truly amazing the emotional power that is generated by a group of passionate people sharing their frustrations and anger apart from prayer and repentance.

Consider some of the horrific things that people have done throughout history when a mob mentality takes over. While I don't want to be too dramatic, I have seen shades of that crazed look at church meetings. You almost expect the deacons to have torches outside the parsonage demanding a little vigilante justice. Another word for this type of emotional frenzy might be *sin*. But that is a question that individual believers must answer for themselves.

I have an acquaintance who has been married four times. His take on that nuptial record? "I guess I'm not very lucky when it comes to marriage." I'll give you luck on the first one, maybe. But somewhere after that second or third divorce, you might want to check out the mirror and see if the problem is staring back at you.

The same principle applies to church schisms. If you have spearheaded (or even participated in) more than one church split, then I can almost certainly suggest the mirror test, and I can probably predict the results of that test if it is honestly applied.

Before you become a participant in a church split, examine your heart. Try to answer these questions honestly:

1. Will this issue matter in eternity?
2. Have I prayed about this?

3. Is it possible that God is teaching me something through this situation and wants me to persevere through it?

4. Is my pride the real issue here? (Even if you built the church, provided 90 percent of the funding, and have attended for 102 years, it is still not *your* church. Acceptance of that truth would mark the end of the Schism Trail in a lot of churches.)

5. Now should I proceed knowing that I might create hurt feelings and possible division?

In the majority of cases, most of us wouldn't get past question one. Few issues that split churches are of eternal consequence. But if the issue involves clear biblical errors in teaching, then you have just cause to proceed on a scriptural path to address the issues.

Whenever people leave a church, I have felt heartbroken. They always espouse rationalizations that sound convincing. But when I ask for specific reasons I generally get a list of problems that are present in 99 percent of churches. Remember, the church is full of sinners, and if they fix that problem, then you and I are both gone.

So if you sense a feeding frenzy starting in your tank, swim away. Stay in the aquarium, but avoid the churning water. Give it some time. Going to church can be like being married. Sometimes it is exciting and fulfilling. Sometimes you hang on only because you have made a commitment to hang on. Until the circumstances that are causing your lack of intimacy are repaired, the relationship won't be the same. Churches, like marriages, have their ups and downs.

Joni and I suffered through one church division in which the pastor left and our church drifted for well over a year with interim leadership. We were tempted to leave, but we stayed for one reason, and I do mean one reason only: Our oldest son was flourishing in the youth ministry after struggling through middle school. So we stayed. The church eventually found a new pastor and then a new worship leader. Now the church is dynamic and growing but, to be honest, we stayed in spite of ourselves.

So in the midst of a frenzy, wait until the ripples settle and the blood is no longer in the water. Then you can make sound judgments. Make sure God is leading you in His will, not in some sort of hypocritical hysteria. I know this sounds harsh, but in the words of my grandpa, "Doggone it! This is important!" After prayer and reflection (and maybe a mirror test), then decide. Leave the church if you must, but make sure in your heart that you go for the right reasons. Be careful about sharing your frustrations with everyone you encounter. Seek the counsel of others you respect who might have a different perspective.

Make genuine efforts to repair relationships whenever you possibly can. Jesus' words in Luke 6:32 convict me about my church relationships: "If you love those who love you, what credit is that to you?" Jesus asked. "Even 'sinners' love those who love them." The truth hurts. But it is still the truth.

I realize that there are times when people feel they must leave a church. When our daughter, Katie, was no longer allowed in our church nursery, Joni and I decided that we had to move on. If our entire family would not be welcomed, we had to find another church home. But we made no attempt to take any other members of the congregation with us. That was private, and God blessed our move.

If my emotions seem a bit raw about this topic, it is because the schisms never seem to end. Since I began writing this book, I have had to revise my earlier numbers. Now seven of the eight churches I have attended have experienced at least some division in the ranks. For the sake of the kingdom, it is time for Christians to get off the Schism Trail. We are needed elsewhere.

Chapter 3

WJSHTOT?

If a dog chases two rabbits, he will never catch one.

—PROVERB

In his book *The Screwtape Letters,* C. S. Lewis puts forth a clever fantasy regarding Satan's strategies with humans. One demon writes to another, "It does not matter how small the sins are provided that their cumulative effect is to edge the man away from the Light and out into the Nothing.... Indeed, the safest road to Hell is the gradual one—the gentle slope, soft underfoot, without sudden turnings, without milestones, without signposts."

I have often considered (with less eloquence than Lewis) what Satan's strategy might be to diminish the effectiveness of Christians. It seems the crux of the strategy to diminish the effectiveness of believers is contained in what I call the 3-D strategy of Division, Diversion, and Derision.

Nothing diminishes the church's effectiveness more than division, as we discussed in chapter 2. Based on personal and painful observation, I believe that division is Satan's most effective strategy.

But when division doesn't work, diversion just might accomplish the same purposes. When we Christians devote our time and energy to anything, even good things, that do not have definite eternal value, then we have been effectively diverted. We will look at the effects of derision in chapter 4. For now, let's take a closer look at diversion.

Diversion comes in many forms. I know whereof I speak, and I must confess that diversion is one of my weaknesses. I am not so prone to division because I tend to be loyal and committed for the long haul. The sports teams that I cheered on as a child are still the ones I follow today. I often try to reason with my wife using this logic: If I never turned my back on the Cleveland Browns, how could I leave you? For reasons beyond my comprehension, this is of little comfort to her. Seriously, I have found better ways to express my devotion to my dear wife, but the fact is, with respect to my church and other commitments, I am loyal and slow to change.

However, my beloved can verify that I am often as easily diverted as a dog at a hydrant factory. Through the years, I have overcommitted time and resources to many pursuits including my work, physical fitness, and coaching the boys' sports teams. None of these things was inherently wrong, but my total immersion in each pursuit caused my faith and my relationships to suffer.

Many Christians suffer from the material diversions of wealth and possessions. Some fall to the diversions of power and prestige. Many succumb to all of the above. But perhaps the most insidious and sobering of Satan's diversions are the good things. Issues that seem important. Things that cause you to want to rise up and fight. But these things can rob our energy and money and time without accomplishing much of anything in light of eternity. And I wonder if your battles and mine don't fall into this category.

The What Would Jesus Do? (WWJD?) phenomenon seems to have peaked (more about that in chapter 10). But this concept in its original form seemed good. Taking a moment to reflect on the Lord's perspective on an action can't be a bad idea. After reflecting on many of the issues that raise our dander and dominate our time, however, I must ask whether we could coin a derivative question: Would Jesus Spend His Time on This? Or, WJSHTOT?

As I first mentioned in chapter 2, we are good at arguing over issues that have little or no eternal value. I think that most Christians can agree upon the gospel: Jesus came to earth, lived a sinless life, and died on the cross as a substitute for each of us. For those of us who believe the gospel to be true, isn't that the key point in all of history? If so, why isn't communicating the gospel to others the number-one priority for *all of us?*

Before Chuck Colson (whom I greatly respect and admire) makes me a *Breakpoint* radio target, I want to stress that certain worldview issues and concerns certainly do merit our resources, time, and attention. The sanctity and dignity of each life, for example, is nonnegotiable to a follower of Christ. Equal but not preferential treatment of the Christian faith in the public arena is worth the battle. Establishing the value of the family is critical to a healthy culture. On issues such as these, Christians must be steadfast and unflinching in their views. (I'll discuss some of those critical concerns in chapter 10.)

Even so, it often seems that Christians spend a lot of time chasing two rabbits and catching none. Case in point: Recently two obviously motivated and concerned Christian women in the small town of Washington, Indiana, went about the task of raising three thousand dollars. They used the money to purchase 273 hardcore pornographic videos for the sole purpose of destroying them. A crowd of a couple hundred cheered and prayed as a highway construction worker pulverized the videos with an asphalt-paving machine. "This was a moral statement we wanted to make," one of the ladies told reporters. My question is simple: What exactly was that moral statement? That pornography is bad? I don't think their gesture contributed much to a belief that is already held by nearly all Christians. It's my guess that non-Christians simply didn't care or watched with disdain.

What did the women accomplish? The videos' vendors, producers, and actors made a profit from the protest purchase. Those outside the faith wondered why Christians would throw away money on such a misguided mission. Christ's message of love for the sinner was not a part of this well-intentioned but misguided diversion. The same amount of money spent to help people addicted to pornography would have been more likely to reap the eternal benefits these dear ladies undoubtedly sought. Make no mistake about it, pornography is sexual heroin. But these women, no matter how well intentioned, merely created a diversion. At the heart of Christ's message is redemption, not condemnation. Those caught in the addiction of pornography already know its destructive and demeaning power. They needed to see the hope of escape through Christ, not demolished videocassettes.

So how can we prevent good intentions from being mere diversions? I believe we need to exercise a fourth D, discernment, by asking ourselves—personally and corporately—questions like these: Will this cause or action count for eternity? Will it communicate the love of Christ and grace of our God to the unchurched? Is this cause important enough to divert my time and energy away from serving others? Would Jesus spend *His* time on this?

Given my propensity to become unbalanced with my time and emotional commitments, I have learned the hard way that I must be discerning. There was a time when I easily rationalized my previously mentioned diversion of chasing success. But the result of my obsession was a period of spiritual drought that, not surprisingly, impacted my marriage as well. Here are a few disciplines that will help us become more discerning.

1. *First and foremost, pray.* I actually hesitate to mention prayer first on such a list because doing so has nearly become cliché. Prayer is only effective, however, when we take the time to seek God and listen to the quiet voice of His Spirit. Too often our prayers are suggestions we make to God about how He should bless our brilliant plans to help Him out. But prayer is not like a pro wrestling match where you know the result before you start.

2. *Study the Bible.* If you spend time studying the methods and ministries of Christ and His apostles, you will get a pretty good set of guidelines for your actions. I would also suggest that one of the most common and dangerous mistakes Christians make is taking a single Bible verse out of context to justify their actions. Avoid this pitfall by using complete texts and contexts to evaluate your circumstances and questions.

3. *Seek the counsel of other Christians, especially those who have walked with the Lord for many years.* I would also encourage you to seek wisdom from believers who are different from you. Just as we often "suggest" instead of pray, we also can line up "counselors" whom we know will be in agreement with our desires. Without diversity of counsel, we risk making errors in judgment.

Paul wrote to the Philippians about seeking discernment: "And this is my prayer: that your love may abound more and more in knowledge and depth of insight, so that you may be able to discern what is best and may be pure and blameless until the day of Christ, filled with the fruit of righteousness that comes through Jesus Christ—to the glory and praise of God" (1:9-11).

As I write this chapter, the holy days in Texas are beginning. Yes, it is football season, and already this season has been notable for unusual reasons. This year's controversy in Santa Fe, Texas, has not been over the coach's offensive strategy, but over one's right to have a public prayer before the game. There is much about the case to raise the hackles of the average concerned Christian. The prayer in question was student-led and had no official endorsement from the administration. What could be the harm in that?

One Texan who supported the high-school prayer was quoted in the *New York Times* as saying, "It's not about praying anymore. It's about our rights and freedoms being taken away." Those are fightin' words for Americans. We care deeply (thank God) about such things. We cared enough to leave countries where state-sanctioned religions forced our ancestors to these very shores to be able to worship as they chose. Do you see the irony here? The United States was founded on the principle that we would not have to listen to state prayers at a public event. (This is where I hope you either read my total context or you can't find my address.) I understand that the Santa Fe prayer was not state sanctioned. I realize that the Christians defending the pregame prayer held an arguably correct position. But was this brouhaha worth it for eternity? Please understand that I totally support the right of the students to pray, and, frankly, nobody can stop them. They don't need a public address system to accomplish their goal.

Another example. Christians have different philosophies about saying grace in a restaurant. Some merely bow silently and thank God in their hearts and mind. Some bow and offer a theatrical and long-winded prayer that should have an intermission. I have seen waiters stand with the iced tea pitcher for minutes wondering if a plague would descend if they filled iced tea glasses during the pharisaical filibuster. But I have never seen a single Christian march to the waiting area, grab the microphone used for reservation announcements, and say grace over the public address system: "Bow with me now as I thank God for these chalupas I am about to consume." You would be stunned. (I would be amused, but I'm not normal.)

The fact is that prayer can't be stopped. Not by government, school boards, the ACLU, tyrants, Norman Lear, the evil media, or any other earthly force. We have the power of prayer as an inheritance from our Lord, and we don't need the validation of nine old justices in robes. I remember a story about a little boy who was misbehaving. His father told him to sit down. He stood up. Dad took him outside for a little reinforcement of the directive. When they came back in, he asked the little boy to sit down again. He did, but with a defiant smile on his face. "What are you smiling about?" Dad asked. The boy answered smugly. "I'm sitting down with my body, but I'm standing up in my heart."

I don't think the Santa Fe protest was a bad thing, and I certainly don't mean to suggest that the people in that fine town had anything other than pure intentions. (I reserve the right to question the motives of some of the out-of-towners who chose to get involved.) But my point is simply this: Did the issue possess eternal significance that would have warranted the energy, time, and other resources spent on it? Would Jesus have spent His time on this?

Again, good things can be diversions. And diversions can keep us from staying on task. And being on task for a Christian is growing in Jesus, loving your neighbor, and sharing the good news of the gospel via your life and words (in that order).

I would suggest that there are far more important issues facing the church than a corporate prayer before a high-school game. Asking the simple question "Would Jesus Spend His Time on This?" could stop many Christian campaigns in their tracks.

One event that might not have passed the WJSHTOT? test was the infamous Disney boycott. In 1996 the Southern Baptist Convention (and later the Assemblies of God) voted to implement a boycott of Disney. The Baptists' list of grievances against the corporate giant was put forth in a resolution that was arguably light on factual information. The SBC stated that Disney hosted gay theme nights at the park, thus implying sponsorship and endorsement of the homosexual lifestyle. The theme park, plus Universal Studios, Sea World, and many other Orlando entertainment venues, are, in fact, all a part of an annual early June gathering called Gay Days. I would agree that families should be aware that these activities are taking place before planning vacations and that the information should be readily available from Disney. That weekend would not be my choice to visit. But I wouldn't want to take a young family to the beach during an MTV Spring Break party either.

I knew one family that supported the Disney boycott but decided to go to the Magic Kingdom anyway because they had nonrefundable tickets. Apparently convictions are more valid when refundable. Another friend of mine was gung-ho in support of the boycott until he realized that ESPN was a Disney company. When his sports ox was gored, he realized that he was giving up not just Bambi but also *Sports Center.* Suddenly he realized that the boycott would cost him something. And isn't that the way so many of us operate? It is easy to be strident when no personal sacrifice is asked or required.

Disney opponents also circulated a petition addressed to Walt Disney president Michael Eisner. The letter stated that "allowing" a gay and lesbian day served as "a clear endorsement of the radical gay agenda by your company." I think instead it demonstrates a clear endorsement of making money from any large group that has a supply of same. For example, Disney has noted that evangelicals have a couple of denarii to rub together as well. The park has sponsored A Night of Joy Christian music celebration since the early 1980s. About three-quarters of a million people have attended these concerts over the years, and this year (2001) featured many of today's top Christian artists. So are we boycotting Disney or not?

The petition goes on to somewhat hysterically decry how Disney "allowed the organizers of Gay and Lesbian Day to portray such beloved Disney characters as Mickey Mouse and Donald Duck as homosexual lovers." Come on, folks. Should we be so worried about two mice (Mickey and Minnie) living together in an undetermined relationship, with a stupid dog (Goofy) and an unintelligible duck (Donald) as friends and another dog (Pluto) who is merely a pet? The whole thing is unstable to begin with. Really—would Jesus spend His time on this?

These petitions were made available via e-mail so that outraged Christians could attach their name and then forward the same message verbatim. I know that boilerplate protest letters increase volume, but does that impress corporate leaders who get the same letter fifty thousand times with just a different name attached? I know it would inspire me to set up an automatic delete function. If you decide to protest an issue because you honestly believe Jesus would have, at least take the time to write an original letter in your own words. Would Jesus have wasted His time forwarding to the Roman senators a protest papyrus with His name attached?

Would Jesus have joined the Disney boycott? Actually, I think He might well have been at Disneyland during Gay and Lesbian Day—and not out of concern for the misrepresentation of Mickey and Donald.

Every day so many good things confront us that can be diversions from the *best* thing God would have each of us do. Like proclaiming the good news of the gospel. As each of us seeks to serve our Lord, I would encourage you to remember the little screening process that will help us weigh the merits of an issue before we act upon it.

Pray. Have a biblical basis.

Seek wise counsel from mature believers.

And ask yourself, *Would Jesus spend His time on this?*

Chapter 4

Fear Christianity

I do not believe in an afterlife, although I am bringing a change of underwear.

—WOODY ALLEN

Had he appeared in our streets today, Chicken Little would have been embraced as a marketing genius, not scorned as an ignored alarmist. Generating fear seems to be the preferred method of commanding the attention of our message-weary populace. Passionate people with a cause rely on fear to impact others. Environmentalists, for example, have always predicted imminent environmental apocalypse if we don't adopt their recommendations. Special interest groups create a fear of hamburgers, arsenic in drinking water, nuclear waste, cell phone radiation, SUVs, hormones in chicken, Teletubbies, pesticides on fruit—you get the idea. The list could on for page after page.

Christians, too, excel at brewing up a good batch of fear. I saw this cheery sign recently posted outside a local church: *Exposure to the Son may prevent burning.* Nothing like a little humorous eternal-damnation pun to bring 'em in. I was raised in a church environment where the standard scare-them-temporarily-straight evangelism method was the top-rated tactic. Our little church featured an altar call every Sunday to coerce into salvation the same three or four unsaved sinners who possessed the courage to attend every week. Our pastor always seemed to personally know someone who had wavered about making a commitment to Christ and then was flattened by a steamroller on his way home from church. Of course, that poor pancaked sinner went to hell because of his stubbornness (and his incredible misfortune to encounter a steamroller on Sunday). The pastor would then give us a taste of eternity by singing seventy or eighty verses of "Just As I Am."

In one memorable service, a church lady tried from verses forty to fifty to persuade me to go to the altar. From verse fifty on she actually tried to physically pull me there. It had to be a comical sight. I resisted like a dog being dragged into the vet for its shots. She finally gave my unrepentant soul over to the steamroller and left me alone. God in His infinite and amazing grace worked in my heart and (without dragging) later brought me to Him. I have always been personally thankful that I came to faith out of conviction and need, not out of fear of damnation and steamrollers. For me, I am not sure that faith based on fear would have survived the long haul.

BURN, BABY, BURN

Fear is the unfortunate ace card of too many evangelistic approaches. I suppose that some people have come to Christ because of the infamous Chick gospel tracts that feature images of people suffering hideously in hell. But I would have to side with Albert Einstein on this particular point. "If people are good only because they fear punishment and hope for reward," he said, "then we are a sorry lot indeed." If Christians can offer no other reason to come to Christ than to avoid hell, then we, too, are a sorry lot indeed. Real faith offers so much more than a get-out-of-hell card in the game of life.

But fear works on the human psyche, so it is easy to exploit. One organization that uses fear and alarmist techniques to excess is People for the Ethical Treatment of Animals (PETA). I find PETA's efforts particularly repulsive. Recently they passed out "Unhappy Meals" at fast-food restaurants. Inside were pictures of slaughtered cows and graphic depictions of what happens in the poultry processing industry. Their message might well have been valid. I personally could not focus on it because of the outrageous and offensive approach. PETA followed that campaign with an invasive billboard showing New York Mayor Rudy Guilliani with the despicable slogan "Got Prostate Cancer?" It was a tasteless attempt to link dairy products to Mr. Guilliani's recently disclosed illness. I was appalled. Again, the message may have been valid. As a forty-something male I am very interested in information that points the way to cancer prevention, but the offensive nature of this attempt to create fear drove me away.

It is particularly disturbing that the church has created its own versions of PETA tactics, and the result has obscured the message of Christ. I am pro-life because of my faith. I believe in the sanctity of life, that it is precious and God given. But I would not be persuaded to hear the pro-life argument if my primary exposure to it came in the form of graphic placards showing bloody, dismembered fetuses being paraded outside an elementary school. We need to be informed about the brutality of abortion techniques and the potential emotional consequences of any abortion. We absolutely need to argue the value of life from a biblical perspective. But I do not want elementary-aged students exposed to such horrifying images that are apparently endorsed (in the minds of the unchurched) by Christians.

Consider the gruesome Christian versions of haunted houses that purport to show what it will be like in hell. One church in Colorado has made an industry out of their Hell House "outreach." Their Web site claims, "Hell House is an exciting, contemporary, timely vehicle that tells in dramatic fashion the timeless message that Jesus is the Way, the Truth, and the only Life. Groups of twenty to twenty-five people will tour Hell House with their own personal demon acting as their tour guide." Stop! Your own personal demon? Move over PETA—you guys are amateurs. "In Hell the tour meets Satan himself. Hell will be hot, smoky, loud, visually disturbing, and sensually confusing." To me that sounds like Las Vegas, but I digress. It gets worse. Here is what you see for your admission ticket of seven dollars a head (no tipping your personal demon). Again quoting from the Hell House Web site:

Scene 1: A funeral scene of a homosexual teenaged boy who has died of AIDS

Scene 2: A riveting reenactment of an abortion

Scene 3: A satanic ritual involving a human sacrifice

Scene 4: A drunk driving accident in which a father realizes he has just killed his own family

Scene 5: A teen-suicide

Scene 6: The sights, sounds, and smells [whatever that might be] of hell and Satan himself.

Eventually the tourists are rescued out of hell by an angel who escorts them to heaven, where they are told the gospel.

As I look over those scenes, I marvel that we worry about the purported offenses of Disney. If you want your own version of this Unhappy Meal, you can order the Hell House Outreach kit for only $199. You'll receive a three-ring binder production manual, a video, and a special-effects CD that includes the voice of God. But to really do it right, you'll want to order some additional resources. For fifteen dollars you can get the human sacrifice background track. (I wish I was making this up.) Other CDs include Hell Screams, which is described as "73 minutes of screaming, groaning, and agonizing sounds of people in torment in hell. Your hell-dwellers will love you for helping them vocally." Your hell-dwellers? There is also a date-rape-scene package and a party-scene package with a character named Pat "Say-jack-you-up," an apparent and somewhat bizarre reference to the *Wheel of Fortune* game show host. And of course you will want to outfit the staff in denim or polo shirts embroidered with the official Hell House Outreach logo.

Satan is real, and we all are participants in an ongoing spiritual battle. But is this really necessary? Is this any better than PETA's "Jesus was a vegetarian" billboards?

AND NOW, A WORD FROM OUR SPONSORS

Fear as an evangelism technique has questionable long-term results. I do not have the resources to do an exhaustive study, but I have talked to a sobering number of people who came to faith out of fear and have yet to experience the liberating wonder of grace. Faith based on fear has the potential of being like a marriage based on abuse. You may hang in with the relationship, but you miss the intended blessings. A seeker brought to faith out of fear had better be quickly instructed in the grace of God if he or she is to grow in Christ.

Fundamentalist Christians (or the religious right) are much maligned in our society—and much of the reputation is earned. The word *fundamentalist* has become a pejorative among many unchurched folks and former churchgoers. In the course of doing research for this book, I sat down at the computer and began to examine the perception of fundamentalist Christians. Dozens of anti-Christian sites later I was stunned, amazed, disturbed, and frankly discouraged by the amount of venomous verbiage directed toward Christians.

What really hurt was the number of sites where former Christians expressed their anger at the church and the faith. I was particularly affected by the comments of those wounded former believers who once stood with us in faith. Criticism is rarely fun, and we tend to view critics in the same way a park statue views a pigeon. But maybe we should see if there is something to be learned. Just the names of the sites are sobering. The following are just a sampling (believe me) of the scores of Internet sites where former Christians air their anger and frustration.

Leaving Born-Again Christianity (http://www. greywlf.com). Discover how the born-again fundamentalist spin on Jesus Christ has fooled people into believing it is the one and only true religion.

Lee Adams Young's Page for Recovering Fundamentalists (http://members.aol.com/ recover2/home.htm). Fundamentalists Anonymous are welcome here. If you have walked away from biblical fundamentalism, these pages suggest how you can still love God, Jesus, and yourself, and respect the Bible.

EX-TIAN Home Page (http://www.infidels.org/ electronic/email/ex-tian/). The home page of the EX-TIAN, the mailing list for and about ex-Christians. Topics include coming out of the closet as an ex-Christian, dealing with family, the holidays, etc. Includes subscription info as well as lots of stories from ex-fundamentalists and some essays.

Walk Away (http://www.berkshire.net/~ifas/wa/). *Walk Away* is a response to numerous requests for support services for ex-fundamentalists...support for those wrestling with the fear and guilt often associated with Christian fundamentalism.

Sites like these will elicit a variety of reactions from Christians. But my heart was troubled. I decided to see what they were saying. Remember, these are men and women who at one time might have sat right behind you at church. They might have proclaimed the name of Jesus as their Savior, but now they use phrases like *recovering from religious abuse*. While our reaction might be to dip into our grab bag of labels (backsliders, sinners) or write-offs (not really a Christian), I encourage you to sprinkle some tenderizer on your heart and listen to these voices.

> Your mind is made up for you, and a set of pre-
> packaged values and opinions are supplied [to] you,
> like a uniform and field pack in basic training.
> (Robert M. Price, from *Fundamentalism to*
> *Humanist*)

Like overprotective parents, we Christians find it easy to jump into the lives of those new to the faith and dictate their lives, just as Robert describes. We must pray for wisdom and restraint in order to allow God to work in a person's life. It's too easy to focus on our agenda (quit smoking, stop cursing, stop everything) and squelch the Spirit of God, who might want to work on a far more important issue.

Besides, Moses wandered in the desert for forty years, yet we want to see maturity in new believers within weeks. I have learned that I must step back, gently advise, support, and allow new Christians to grow at their own pace. God knows how to grow His sheep. No amount of flailing them with our Shepherd's staff will expedite the process. I am sorry for all believers who were not given the opportunity to grow in faith at their own pace. Faith is real. Faith has worked for me. But my faith did not mature overnight.

> The most annoying thing is that all the people who
> used to be my fellow Xians and used to believe that
> I was as good as the rest of them explained my

losing-of-my-faith away by claiming that I "probably never had any faith anyway" or "it's just a
rough period, you'll return to Jesus." I know that
for that period of my life I had absolute faith and
devotion and then to be told that you probably
didn't is insulting. (Ben Creagh Brown)

I know I have been guilty as charged by Ben. I apologize to
you for the clichéd response. I hope you will someday desire to
reexamine the faith and that you will find more support from your
fellow Christians.

I've felt religious euphoria many times before. This
is the first time that I'd ever felt real PEACE. Gone
is the fear of eternal damnation, the weariness of
working for heaven. Once those things are gone,
the rest of Christianity, with its glittering edifices of
rationalization, all comes crashing down. (Jason
Steiner, from the EX-TIAN archives)

In the words of comedian Chris Rock (please, hold your
e-mails), "I'm not saying it's right, but I understand." The crash from
religious euphoria is much like coming down from the euphoria of
romantic infatuation. I don't feel the same giddy infatuation that I
had when Joni and I first fell in love. But my feelings for her are so
much deeper and real after twenty-five years of growing and working out the relationship. On the days when I don't "feel" love, I realize my commitment to her. The feelings return. And they will leave
again. Ideally, our faith should follow that model. Sadly, Jason did

not experience the peace that I have found in my faith. That he believes his lack of peace was in part the result of other Christians should cause us concern. Jason's other comments break my heart. The fear of eternal damnation and the weariness of working for heaven are two burdens that a Christian should never have to carry. I understand his feelings and where they came from. But that is not what Christ intends for His followers.

> [I now have g]reater interest in and enjoyment of things around me (such as science, music, art, nature, etc.). Enjoyment of such things was discouraged when I was in church—they said we shouldn't get too enamored [with] the things of this world, since heaven is our real home. (from the EX-TIAN mailing list)

I believe you experienced this—but which church did you attend? Come visit us at our church, and you can freely enjoy all of these things or your money back.

> I feel freer to try things and even make mistakes, since I don't worry about a God watching me and threatening me with punishment or misfortune. (from the EX-TIAN mailing list)

This is the same kind of church atmosphere I was exposed to while growing up. When my church sang about amazing grace, the amazing part was if you found grace anywhere. Then I learned about grace, and my entire perspective on faith changed, albeit slowly. I can assure you that God is not watching anxiously for you to stumble so He can rain affliction on you.

> [I have m]ore ability to make friends of other beliefs
> and backgrounds—before, such friendships were
> discouraged since those people were "of the devil"
> and "might lead us away from Christ." (from the
> EX-TIAN mailing list)

Good thing Jesus didn't go to this church. We wouldn't be having this little talk today. I heartily recommend making friends with those people "of the devil." Who knows, you might lead them toward Christ. Just keep a balance in your relationships. Relationships exclusively outside the faith might not be best for your spiritual health. But believe me, relationships exclusively within the faith will put you in violation of the Great Commission as well. In the heart of a follower of Christ, there is no place for a fear of unbelievers.

A FEAR OF OUR OWN

For many years a big part of my personal fear of unbelievers was a lack of confidence in my intellectual position as a Christian. I feared intellectual embarrassment. I feared that I could not adequately defend my beliefs. According to some critics, the average Christian would have to be tutored extensively just to be dumb as a rock. Most of us don't enjoy being perceived as stupid. As for me, I have kids to fulfill that need in my life.

Actually, being perceived as stupid would be getting off light according to many. Here are some quotes from really smart guys that I once found intimidating. But confronting my doubts and intellectual fears has allowed me to address these critics with confidence that my faith will not be diminished. Isaac Asimov, in the *Canadian Atheists Newsletter,* says:

> Imagine the people who believe such things and who are not ashamed to ignore, totally, all the patient findings of thinking minds through all the centuries since the Bible was written. And it is these ignorant people, the most uneducated, the most unimaginative, the most unthinking among us, who make themselves the guides and leaders of us all; who would force their feeble and childish beliefs on us; who would invade our schools and libraries and homes.

Good thing I am too stupid to be offended. The intellectual arrogance of Asimov is staggering. But his point about how we force our beliefs is worth examining. I have found that when I am living in fellowship with Christ, doors open as if on their own; I can leave my evangelistic battering ram at home. Evangelism is not effective when forced.

Another ringing endorsement comes from the ever upbeat Bertrand Russell.

> There is something feeble and a little contemptible about a man who cannot face the perils of life with-

out the help of comfortable myths. Almost
inevitably, some part of him is aware that they are
myths, and that he believes them only because they
are comforting. But he dares not face this thought!
Moreover, since he is aware, however dimly, that his
opinions are not rational, he becomes furious when
they are disputed.

Thanks, Bertrand! It is always nice to know what I am thinking (however dimly) in my mythical little world. What a backbreaking load of assumptions Mr. Russell unloaded in that paragraph. Again, however, there is a point worth taking with us. Don't get furious when someone disputes your faith. A secure follower of Christ can respond with assurance and dignity, and without arrogance. You don't have to agree with something to give it the courtesy of respect. In *Mere Christianity*, C. S. Lewis illustrated the search for truth this way: "If you are a Christian, you are free to think that all those religions, even the queerest ones, contain at least some hint of truth.... But, of course, being a Christian does mean thinking that where Christianity differs from other religions, Christianity is right and they are wrong. As is arithmetic—there is only one right answer to a sum, and all other answers are wrong; but some of the wrong answers are much nearer being right than others."

You can't lovingly discuss the gospel with another human while denigrating their beliefs or values. Consider your own reactions to Asimov's and Russell's comments above. I can pretty much guarantee that if you do so, you won't have an open-minded audience.

The philosopher Friedrich Nietzsche has influenced much of modern thought. He was a bitter foe of Christianity, as witnessed by statements like this:

> The Christian resolution to find the world ugly
> and bad has made the world ugly and bad.

Didn't realize how much power we had, did you? Remember when we passed that Christian resolution (Sin Bill 207-B)? Just out of curiosity, in those places where Christianity has no influence, how in the world did folks figure out how to be ugly and bad all by their good-hearted selves?

Evolutionary biologist Ernst Mayr noted:

> There is nothing that supports the idea of a
> personal God.

Nothing? Not one shred of evidence that would demand at least a cursory investigation? That is a bold and authoritative-sounding statement from a real smart guy. But it discounts as rubbish the anecdotal experience of millions of honest and intelligent people. All deluded? What are the odds of that? Mr. Mayr has summarily concluded that even a cynical guy like me can be brainwashed and manipulated for three decades into believing in something that has no support. I beg to differ.

It is easy to experience intellectual intimidation when so many elite thinkers denigrate faith. But then there is always the possibility articulated by Claude McDonald that "sometimes a majority simply means that all the fools are on the same side." While the

Christian intellectual position has not always been brilliantly orchestrated, even scientists can be (brace yourselves) wrong. In 1872, a French professor of physiology at Toulouse sniffed that "Louis Pasteur's theory of germs is ridiculous fiction." And Albert Einstein was, by all accounts, smarter than the average guy, but even he had some embarrassing moments. "There is not the slightest indication that nuclear energy will ever be obtainable," he said in 1932. "It would mean that the atom would be shattered at will."

The arrogant and closed-minded statements about Christianity presented earlier are as detrimental as statements like, "God said it, I believe it, and you had better believe it too—or you're going to hell!" Neither approach is a safe springboard to open discussion.

Christians have an important message: Real faith works. But the means of communicating it are vital. Fear should not be a tactic in a Christian's arsenal. The apostle John summarized it beautifully:

> In this way, love is made complete among us so that
> we will have confidence on the day of judgment,
> because in this world we are like him. There is no
> fear in love. But perfect love drives out fear, because
> fear has to do with punishment. The one who fears
> is not made perfect in love. We love because he first
> loved us. (1 John 4:17-19)

In the movie *A League of Their Own,* baseball manager Jimmy Dugan (played by Tom Hanks) tries to adjust to managing a women's team during World War II. When one of his players breaks down in tears, he looks at her in amazement and proclaims, "There's no crying in baseball!" Christians need to be just as sure to proclaim, "There's no fear in love!" The gospel of Christ will always be offensive to some, but we must admit that we can do better in how we communicate the gospel. We must do better. With Him. With grace.

Without fear.

Chapter 5

Whose Idea Was This?

Driving home from church, Mrs. Johnson asked her husband,
"Did you see that the Smiths' daughter pierced her eyebrow?"
"I didn't notice her," Mr. Johnson said.
"And how about Rita Jones? Could you believe how short her
dress was?" Mrs. Johnson continued. "The nerve of a Sunday-
school teacher to wear such an immodest outfit."
"I guess I didn't notice that either," Mr. Johnson confessed.
"For goodness sake!" Mrs. Johnson exclaimed. "A lot of good
it does for you to go to church."
—http://www.cleanjokespage.com

On April 22, 1985, the world's leading soft-drink producer decided to change what had made them number one for decades. That day the marketing genius of the Coca-Cola Company debuted New Coke to the great consternation of millions of devoted Coke drinkers. A friend of mine hoarded a basement full of cases of old Coke. Presumably he would sit there with his shotgun as desperate Coca-Cola junkies tried to storm his mother lode. By July of that same year, the company had apologized and reintroduced the old product, now dubbed Coke Classic. The whole process had the vast majority of Americans asking the simple question, "What in the world were they thinking?"

The same question crosses my mind when I think about God's marketing plan for Christianity. Why in the world would a God who created the heavens and the earth decide to use people like Jim Bakker and Jimmy Swaggart and me to represent Him? Wouldn't a couple of miracles or direct communications in the clouds be more effective? As Woody Allen once said, "If only God would give us some clear sign! Like making a large deposit in my name at a Swiss bank."

In our culture the word *marketing* has taken on a negative connotation. Marketing now is lumped in with bad words like *media* and *politicians*. Marketing, however, simply means the process of promoting a product or service. Christianity has one message that is paramount, and that is the gospel of Jesus Christ, the good news that God has provided a way for us to have an actual relationship with Him. But our marketing has been about as focused as Mr. Magoo wielding a manual-focus camera.

If the creative types on Madison Avenue had been entrusted with the task of marketing Christianity, they probably would have tried to talk God into something a little different.

THE OFFICES OF SLICK, SHALLOW, & TRITE
AGENCY: Okay, God, You've got a great concept. Great upside. Good branding, and Your recognition rating is out of sight. But we have a big problem.

GOD: Problem?

SS&T: Yeah, You've pretty much left all of Your marketing to Your people, these…whaddya call 'em…Christians.

GOD: Yes.

SS&T: It's not working, Big Guy. These Christian people have given You a really bad image problem. I think we need to rethink this whole Christian marketing thing. You know…think outside the box…be creative.

GOD: Ever seen a giraffe?

SS&T: Yeah, yeah. Whatever. Wait. I've got it! We change the name. The branding of "Christian" is just not reaching the demographic we're after.

GOD: You mean sinners?

SS&T: Sinners? Whoa, Big Guy. Lighten up! Are You kidding me? Drop that like a hot coal. Nobody wants to be called sinners anymore. It diminishes their self-esteem. Creates a bad karma.

GOD: Easy…

SS&T: Whatever. Here's what our creative team rec-
ommends. We lower the bar a bit on all these rules.
A couple of those commandments are a little rough.
I mean, we're all pretty much good with murder and
stealing, but some of these others are...well, a bit old
school. Let's make it more "feel good." Create some
synergy between the faith and nature. We'll bring in
some pros to be Your reps. People who can communicate and look good. Improve the image. A few
miracles would be nice, but we need to package that
in a network special during prime time. How about
Pestilence and Vengeful Acts of God on Fox? We'll roll
out the whole campaign at the Super Bowl with a
USA Today insert. And let's drop this Christian title.
How about "Humans of Faith"? That has a nice
inclusive ring to it. We can have Humans of Faith
rallies. Let me show You this logo we mocked up—

GOD: I think I'll stay with the original plan.

SS&T: Hey, whatever. Don't blame us when You
have to reorganize. You'll see who's right.

GOD: I know.

WHAT'S IN A NAME?

It is interesting to note that in the early church the followers of
Jesus were first known as disciples. The term *Christian* is not men-

tioned until Acts 11:26. Many believe the term actually came from the unbelievers in the city of Antioch in their efforts to describe this radical new group. In any case, it stuck.

A big problem in our marketing of the faith has been the devaluation of the name *Christian*. Many believers have adopted "followers of Christ" to try to distance themselves from the confusion. Actually, the definition of *Christian* has become so generic that it is almost meaningless in identifying the real article. The label is used as often to describe a "good" person as it is to identify a disciple of Jesus Christ. But many "good" people do not associate themselves with Christ at all. Ironically, but equally problematic, Christianity is also frequently linked to hate groups and the lunatic fringe, even though such people clearly do not follow the teachings of Christ.

According to the polls, nearly fifty million people in our country call themselves evangelical Christians. I would suggest that there are far fewer people who should claim the title than the polls suggest. If those fifty million people really understood and lived something close to the teachings of Christ, would our nation be in such moral decline? If we really believed and lived according to what we say we believe, would the difference not be profound?

Recently I have become aware of the importance that corporations place on how their product is perceived. In 1999, the Pizza Hut chain sued another pizza chain for misleading advertising and product claims. Pizza Hut sued Papa Johns for making the claim that Papa Johns had "Better ingredients, Better pizza." I was astounded. Pizza Hut was concerned about that? I don't know how things work at your house, but with us advertising claims work only once. If I like Pizza Hut products better than the pizza from

Papa Johns, my decision is made. Papa Johns could tell me their pizza would double my IQ, and it wouldn't matter. And yet perception mattered so much to Pizza Hut that they sued!

Unfortunately, unlike the major corporations, there are no trademark lawyers fighting for the integrity of the Christian label. In our society, lawyers earn a good living making sure you use brand names correctly. You must say *photocopy* instead of Xerox when speaking of making paper reproductions. Xerox rightly does not want to lose the integrity of their brand name. Lawyers will contact you for using *Kleenex* as a generic term for tissue. The integrity of a name is vital to a company's survival. But the integrity of the word *Christian* has been so sadly compromised that anyone can use the title, no questions asked.

That strikes me as being patently unfair. Wearing fatigues doesn't make me a war veteran. Wearing Nikes and the number 23 doesn't make me play like Michael Jordan. Yet Christians are the targets of religious profiling, a spiritual bigotry as unfair as any other form of racism. Everyone given the name gets tossed into the same stereotypical dumpster. You have a church or group. Jesus is mentioned. You are a Christian. And the cynical response goes something like this:

"So you're a Christian, huh? You one of those abortion clinic–bombing, gay-hating, sexually repressing, censoring bigots that I hear so much about?"

NO, I AM NOT!

I am a seeker of truth. I have come to a considered decision that Jesus Christ is the best path to truth. I abhor abortion, yet at the same time I am appalled by the heavy-handed, loveless, and unbiblical techniques that zealots use to protest it. I believe that the gay lifestyle is not scriptural, but I know that every gay man and woman is a creation of the loving God and deserves my love and compassion. I believe that pornography is profoundly dangerous, and I grieve for the victims of this perverted industry. I detest much of the current thought and cultural direction, but I do not believe that censorship is the answer. What I do believe is that genuine Christians need to summon the courage to live a different and attractive lifestyle that will actually offer an alternative to honest seekers of truth.

I wish we could hire a high-powered law firm to intimidate and litigate against everyone who uses the term "Christian" when that group demonstrates none of the fruits of a relationship with Christ. Most of these groups are better described as being merely religious. If we must use *gelatin* instead of Jell-O, how about protecting the brand name *Christian?* If you ain't livin' the life, you are just religious. My attorneys will be in touch.

NO FRUIT IN THIS PRODUCE STAND— BUT THERE ARE A LOT OF NUTS!

Next to the merely religious, we have the merely religious nuts, who also claim to follow the teachings of Christ. They can be harmless and silly, like the Internet site offering ten dollar "tickets to heaven" admitting one person to the afterlife (group rates not available). Religious zealots can be a little (or a lot) frightening. Have you heard about those groups dedicated to training the American "Christian remnant" about our "duty" to be armed? The following excerpt came from a sermon delivered by Pastor John Stephen Brown of the Eternal Grace Baptist Church. He was commenting on the tragic shootings at Wedgewood Baptist Church in Fort Worth, Texas. I am quoting this as printed so I will not be accused of changing context. The emphasis in italics is mine.

As a blood bought, born again, baptized believer indwelt by the Holy Spirit of God, I am reminded of God's Word in the wake of recent events.

Bible believers are taught by the Word of God to arm themselves and be trained in the use of those weapons. While being properly trained in our weapon of choice, the Holy Bible, we are duty bound to be trained in other weapons of warfare. We understand many are not properly trained in the use of both spiritual and carnal weapons [and only when so trained] can someone be a good steward over the manifold blessings of God.

It is the duty of Pastors, Deacons and Men of the Church to provide protection in the above manner.

I am encouraging all who have repented of their sins and named the name of Christ to deny themselves, and daily bath [sic] their minds in the Word of God. Moreover, I am counseling those believers to properly arm themselves and get appropriate training where necessary. *Had the people in Fort Worth, Texas, faithfully been obeying our LORD's Word, the death toll would have been much less.*

May Christ our Lord be glorified through our thoughts and actions!!!

I am not a gun-control guy. But I step way back when I hear we are "duty bound" to be trained in other weapons of warfare. No wonder the world looks at us suspiciously. Before I move on, I can't let this kind of thinking go unchallenged: How can this pastor lay the blame at the feet of those suffering believers at Wedgewood? How can one respond to such a tragedy with a statement from the pulpit like the "death toll would have been much less" had they "faithfully been obeying our LORD's Word?" I want to say to my brothers and sisters at Wedgewood that your very presence in God's house indicates you were faithfully obeying the Lord's Word. May God give you the peace of knowing you did no wrong.

On a lighter (but still embarrassing) note, religious nuts can be amusing. Consider the Internet site explaining the earth is not moving because the Bible declares the earth to be motionless. Okay. Or they can be just odd…like the man who has carried a twelve-foot wooden cross around the world for nearly thirty years.

They can also be misleading. Benny Hinn is the most flamboyant representative of the signs and miracles movement, a theology based on the power of faith that seems merely to spiritualize the metaphysical "power of the mind" concept and dress it up in Christian language. According to this movement, believers have absolute authority and can claim faith to overcome or prevent illness as well as to generate prosperity and happiness.

The tactics of the televangelists tied to this movement are outrageous, yet they continue to attract a following. The Reverend A. A. Allen asserted he could command God to "turn dollar bills into twenties." As a father with two sons in a private college, I can see why that is an attractive theology, but it is not grounded in the teachings of Christ.

The Trinity Foundation is a watchdog organization that monitors televangelists and the faith movement. They reported one woman received an inheritance of fifty-three thousand dollars, and over time she sent one of these evangelists forty-nine thousand dollars of that money. When hard times came she appealed to his church and was told to go to a social services agency. I'm pretty sure that is not what Jesus would do.

Frederick Price is the self-proclaimed "chief exponent of the Name It and Claim It" theology. He has told his followers that sickness is "not allowed" in his home. His wife, however, has been treated for cancer. Somehow Price claims to drive a Rolls Royce because he is following in Jesus' steps.

Robert Tilton has been the subject of a scathing exposé on ABC's *Prime Time Live*. The show's producers found the prayer request letters he promised to pray over tossed into trash Dumpsters. His response was bizarre at best. Tilton said, "I laid on top of those prayer requests so much that the chemicals actually got into my bloodstream, and…I had two small strokes in my brain."

I am exercising a rare moment of restraint here.

I am hesitant to criticize those who call themselves messengers of God. For one, they don't take criticism well. Consider these comments to and about their critics:

> "Sometimes I wish God will give me a Holy Ghost machine gun; I'll blow your head off." (Benny Hinn)

> "It is a fearful thing to fall into the hands of an angry God! Touch not my anointed! Do my prophets no harm!" (Robert Tilton)

Such threats aside, proclamations of men like these have ranged from outrageous to ridiculous to downright dangerous. I am in no position to judge their salvation or sincerity, only their methods. I sit here looking into a mirror and ask myself, "Who do I think I am casting stones?" But such teachings must be disputed.

The sad fact is that all of these messages contribute to the prevailing negative image of the Christian church that many nonbelievers have. And, brother, what you see ain't what you get when you actually wade into who Jesus is. Even a cursory glance at the life of Christ shows the incongruous nature of most of these wild claims. Christ's teachings were uncomfortable. Edgy. Sacrificial. Following in Jesus' steps would more likely involve selling the Rolls and giving away the money than driving it in His name. But more on that in chapter 11.

Those walking in the faith need to know and understand what Christ taught. Jesus did not promise to eradicate sickness in our lives. Faith will not guarantee prosperity. But a relationship with God will give us something far more precious than wealth or even health. It will give us a purpose for our existence. And it can give peace to our souls.

At the end of your days it will matter not at all what Benny Hinn or Robert Tilton or Dave Burchett believed. All of us could be as wrong as having artificial turf on a major league baseball field. All that matters is this: Who do you say Jesus Christ is? That question must be answered. And it will be answered—by everyone.

GETTING IN SYNC WITH THE BIG IDEA

The sad reality is that the biggest marketing problem for Christianity is not misrepresentation. It is not biased newspapers. It is not "godless" national leaders. The problem is not the pro wrestling division of the faith, more commonly known as televangelists. It is not the evil "media" or television or movies. These are merely symptoms of the biggest problem. The biggest problem in Christianity is found in the local church. It is me. And it may be you.

Many Christians have become so totally assimilated into the culture that there is nothing distinctive about their lives. Others are so unaware of God's grace that they live a life of joyless tedium that is attractive to no one.

Sometimes I wonder what God was thinking when He decided Christians would be His representatives here on earth and often many people's first impression of Jesus Christ. The old cliché that you only have one chance to make a good first impression is never truer than in the church. Could there be a worse marketing campaign than the following headlines generated over the past several years? In no particular order, here is a very short list of a Christian marketing hall of shame.

- Ja'Marc Antoine Davis of the Christian band Raze was arrested and charged with molestation and rape. The band had just begun a thirty-city tour when Davis was arrested.
- Jim and Tammy Faye Bakker bilked millions of dollars out of Christian believers to build their PTL empire. I have personal issues here because my sainted grandmother took in sewing to be a PTL "partner" with Jim and Tammy. Finally PTL went bankrupt in a sea of corruption and misappropriations. Baker served several years in prison. Later he humbly repented and developed a low-key and apparently sincere ministry. But the damage was done.

- Oral Roberts. The venerable television preacher announced that an eight-hundred-foot-tall Jesus had given him a vision to build a hospital in Tulsa. Later God threatened to "call him home" (kill him) if he didn't raise the money to finish the project. Oral's supporters produced, and he built the hospital. Within a few years it went bankrupt. Was Roberts sincerely trying to do the right thing? It doesn't matter. The media was delirious in its eagerness to lampoon the effort.

- Amy Grant and Gary Chapman, two of today's top Christian recording artists, ended their marriage. The public reaction is cynical: There is no difference between them and any other couple. And their point is tough to argue.

- Eugene Robinson, a safety for the Atlanta Falcons football team, won the Athletes in Action "Christian Man of the Year" award and was arrested in a prostitution vice bust that same weekend. Robinson was contrite and apologetic, but no headlines highlighted that part of the story.

- Christian recording artist Michael English was forced to give back his Dove Award after an extramarital affair with another Christian artist destroyed his marriage.

When a Christian scandal explodes, the collateral damage wounds the unaffiliated servants as much as the person at the center of attention. Most of us who identify ourselves as Christians shake our heads and condemn all incidents that damage the cause of Christ. And yet on some level, if not as publicly, we all have failed. We have failed to understand what being a Christian means and what should result from that responsibility. G. K. Chesterton observed correctly that "Christianity has not been tried and found wanting; it has been found difficult and not tried."

As we will discuss in the next chapter, there is a huge difference between "walkin' it and talkin' it." Belief doesn't necessarily result in positive actions. I believe in exercise; I have a harder time with action. We blame the world's problems on everyone and everything from Satan to Hollywood (a redundancy to some readers). And yet *we* have the resources to turn this culture upside down. This truth is sometimes ugly, and it won't set us free until we corporately choose to respond to it. In the immortal words of the cartoon character Pogo, "We have found the enemy and it is us."

So why *did* God choose us to be His messengers? Obviously, when God created humanity with free will, He knew that we would fail. Yet, as an earthly father, I look at my sons and see the potential in them even when they are not fulfilling that potential. I believe that God, in perfect love, looks at me and sees what I can be. He sees far more potential in me than I could even imagine. Am I anything special? Hardly. But God knows what one completely committed believer can do. The catch is that I have to give up my personal agenda, and that is not easy. But I sense that more and more of my generation (the Boomers) are ready for that change. We Baby Boomers have tried nearly everything in our frenetic and often fruitless pursuit of happiness. Now a lot of us are ready to make the rest of our lives count for something other than personal aggrandizement.

God knows what He is doing. He knows His marketing plan has worked. It worked in the early church. It worked during the great revivals of history. God knows His plan will work again. It will take good workers who are ready to make a difference. Whose idea was this? It was, and still is, God's idea. And it will work as soon as we are ready.

Part II

Why Won't Those Heathens Listen?

Thoughts on How We Lost Our Audience

Chapter 6

Our Walkin' Ain't
Matchin' Our Talkin'

*Who you are speaks so loudly I can't hear what you
are saying.*

—RALPH WALDO EMERSON

was shocked to pick up my newspaper and read the headline:

BAPTISTS MORE LIKELY TO DIVORCE THAN ATHEISTS

Excuse me? How can that be? What is wrong with this picture?
How can I talk to people about Jesus making a difference when
Christianity apparently can't even hold a marriage together? I was
further dismayed to read the front page of the *Atlanta Journal
Constitution* (5/23/2000) concerning one of our most revered Christian leaders. The Reverend Charles Stanley of Atlanta's First Baptist Church had just told his congregation that his marriage of
forty-four years was irretrievably broken. The paper pointed out
that Dr. Stanley had told his congregation in 1995, "If my wife
divorces me, I would resign immediately." When Dr. Stanley's wife

filed for divorce five years later, he did not resign. Stanley informed the Baptist Press that the "pledge doesn't apply." Quoting that publication, he stated the pledge was for the particular time and circumstance five years prior, and he had not meant he would necessarily follow through in the future. And that is my issue with Dr. Stanley. I don't know all the details behind his obviously difficult decision to divorce. I do know that he was on record with a statement that he would resign, and he did not.

My point is not to rip Charles Stanley but to illustrate why non-Christians become so cynical. The world is watching us. They are watching and wondering whether we will be different. Too often we are not. At least not so different as to be salty enough to generate a healthy spiritual thirst.

A Dallas sports talk-radio station recently hosted a debate about an athlete who is very vocal about his Christianity. Even so, he is often rude, intimidating, and occasionally profane in his encounters with the media. Yet he expects those same media types to promote his ministry activities. I can't even begin to describe how cynical about Christianity many of these reporters who covered him have become.

THE SOFT HERESY OF LOW EXPECTATIONS

President George W. Bush campaigned heavily on education issues. In Texas he was particularly opposed to the phenomenon known as social promotion, a practice that simply pushes underachieving students through the system whether they have learned anything or not. It is the easiest thing to do. Mr. Bush called it the "soft bigotry of low expectations."

Special-needs students are often the most likely to suffer from this social promotion ideology. From the system's point of view, they are a hassle. I speak from some authority here since Joni works in the special education department of a large Texas school district. I hear the stories and see her frustration. But I also see how much she cares and how much the teachers she works with care. I rejoice with her in the victories and then wonder how much grief and taxpayer money the dedicated and underappreciated educators save with each one. Recently at a local restaurant, I witnessed the reason why Joni keeps trying. We had just sat down to eat when my wife's face lit up. "There's one of my kids!" Joni exclaimed. The boy and his mother came rushing to the table to relate his recent successes. All As and Bs on the last report card. The proud, beaming faces of the student and mom (and my wife) could have lighted the restaurant. This boy had been blessed with a mom and some education professionals who didn't dismiss him with low expectations.

It seems we do the same thing to Christians. If I might modify President Bush's thought, we believers are guilty of a similar dismissal. We are guilty of *the soft heresy of low expectations*. We do not expect the best from our Christian brothers and sisters. We do not demand the best from them or from ourselves.

I must hasten to add that some of us take the equally detrimental approach of expecting nothing short of perfection. A walk of faith with Christ should be characterized neither by low expectations nor by standards of perfection.

Have you ever had a teacher or coach who pushed you past what you thought you were capable of achieving? Chances are good that, at times, you didn't like that teacher or coach. But later you realized what that wise mentor was doing. We often cannot see our own potential as clearly as someone else can.

God sees our potential. And he does not have low expectations for us, but we tend to accept (often with a little help from the brethren) a lowering of the bar.

TOO CLOSE TO HOME?

The Barna Research Group reported that 29 percent of adult Baptists have been through a divorce. Only my demographic (nondenominational churches) had a higher rate at 34 percent. Of major Christian denominations, the Catholics and Lutherans have the lowest rate of divorce, perhaps because they can drink. Regardless, shouldn't a relationship with Christ reduce the divorce rate significantly? It absolutely should. So why aren't we different?

The standard judgmental Christian approach is to rail against sins that are either not a concern for us personally or those that don't wander too close to home. For example, a sin that appalls me is…drumroll, please…crack use. Why? Because I have never had a problem with drugs, and crack users tend to be from a different segment of the population than my own. So I can rail and rail against the evils of crack. Smokers? Feel my wrath. I witnessed the slow death of my stepgrandfather from emphysema and consequently never had a desire to smoke. But my conviction was born out of revulsion at the ugly death of my grandfather more than any upright spiritual convictions. If the conversation moves to caffeine addiction, my fervor goes away, and my profound belief in personal space and the separation of church and Starbucks increases dramatically.

Here is a list of sins that typically appall Christians:

- drugs
- drinking
- smoking
- premarital sex
- extramarital sex
- pornography
- extraterrestrial sex (just seeing if you were paying attention)
- cursing
- homosexuality
- immodest dress

And here is a list of sins that we *should* care about but typically don't because caring might interfere with our daily business:

- gossip
- greed
- selfishness
- materialism
- anger
- bitterness
- pride
- unforgiveness
- racism
- envy
- lust
- sexism
- classism
- indifference
- homophobia

The bottom line is simply this: In our human condition, it is a heck of a lot easier to confess other people's sins than our own. I can spot your sins a mile away in the fog. My own are not as readily apparent to me. I always enjoy when a pastor talks about problems in relationships. Since this doesn't apply to me (note from Joni: "Baloney"), I am free to look around the room. I love to see a husband or wife elbow or nudge the other when a point is made. Call me naive, but it seems to me that a point that has to be elbowed home probably won't take root.

Another aspect of the human condition is our need to compare ourselves to others. This is especially true of the need to find comparisons that support our sense of superiority over someone else. I guarantee you a lot of Christians have compared themselves to me and felt that their own sainthood was imminent. I confess that I have also looked at the lives of other Christians and felt better about my own spiritual walk. I have definitely looked at the messed up lives of unbelievers and felt superior. Is that what Jesus has in mind for me? Hardly.

RIGHT JUDGMENT

When we start looking down our spiritual noses at the lives of others, we are in dangerous waters. I saw a brutally honest T-shirt at a local amusement park. On the front it said, "Jesus Loves You." On the back it said, "But I Don't." We would actually be better off displaying that kind of frankness if our faith has no effect on how we treat those around us. Honestly, how many times have you been just a little more ticked off because a driver with a Christian symbol on his car cut you off in traffic? If the driver had a pentagram on the bumper, you'd be more likely to nod and expect such behavior. Maybe even pray for the lost soul. But you expect Christian drivers to be above reproach. And they are not. One of my major fears in writing this book is that you will raise the bar on my own life. I did wait until I was old enough to have a fighting chance.

Every time you identify your connection to Christ, the bar is in fact raised. Today a policeman turned in front of me without signaling. I was initially angered that he did that. Then I realized that dozens of drivers every week do the same thing and I am not upset. So why was I bothered? My anger stemmed from the officer being a civil hypocrite. He would have demanded that I use my signal and obey the law, yet he didn't follow the rules. I expected more of him because he was a police officer. He *should follow the law* more consistently than I do. The same higher standard applies when we claim the name of Christ. Unfair? Maybe a little. But it is the nature of humanity. Our Christian lives should create interest, not validate cynicism.

I have always been guilty of knee-jerk judgments. I have a tendency to judge people by clothing, occupation, hair, facial hair, voice…you name it. I make Judge Judy look wishy-washy when it comes to quick judgments. As I grow older I am beginning to realize the folly of that approach. I could outline (but won't for obvious reasons) a list of people whom I initially disliked, but who turned out to be wonderful friends. I could also list (and wish my attorney would let me) a ledger of people who impressed me at first glance and turned out to be weasels. The problem is that no one can nor should be judged by a snapshot.

If someone photographed you at random for the cover of a magazine, you would most likely be furious. Your hair could be mussed, your expression likely would be goofy, and your clothing inappropriate. When someone makes a snapshot judgment of you as a Christian, the same thing can happen. You could be having a bad spiritual hair day. Your expression could be grumpy. You might be tired, depressed, or emotionally distraught. Financial pressures could be weighing you down. And on that day, at that moment, your snapshot is hardly cover material. To be fair, snapshot judgments are, in part, responsible for Christians' bad rep with non-Christians. It's not entirely our fault that we are often branded as hypocrites because non-Christians brand us with judgments based on singular events that do not accurately represent our lives. It's human behavior. All that we can do is be aware of our responsibility to represent Christ every time we step out the door.

As Christians, we must take the time to look at the entire album of a person's life. Then we will see enough snapshots to make a valid judgment. You might see that shots of beauty, compassion, and love far outnumber the shots of anger or despair. I am trying to stop making snapshot judgments.

So how do we reconcile the potential conflict between raising expectations among the body of Christ while also avoiding judgmental attitudes toward one another? Good question. First, it seems to me that Christians have taken a verse or two and effectively decided we cannot evaluate the actions of other believers. I always heard the ominous *King James Version,* "Judge not, that ye be not judged!" as the absolute prohibition of judging others. Earlier we discussed the little issue of scriptural context. The entire text of the first and second verses in chapter 7 of Matthew actually says, "Do not judge, or you too will be judged. For in the same way you judge others, you will be judged, and with the measure you use, it will be measured to you." That seems fair enough. If I am going to evaluate (judge) your actions, I should be held accountable to the same standard.

Later in the same passage Jesus lambastes the hypocrites for seeing the speck in their brother's eye when they have a plank in their own. Does Jesus say unequivocally not to evaluate your brothers and sisters? Not at all. Jesus says, "First take the plank out of your own eye, and then you will see clearly to remove the speck from your brother's eye" (verse 5). Jesus teaches that we had better do our own housecleaning before we worry about some dust in someone else's house. Only when we are open to inspection can we see clearly and act rightly in judging the actions of others.

The fact is that we cannot act as God's marketing staff here on earth without the ability to judge actions as wrong. "Actions" is the key word here, since we are given authority to judge only the actions of others in light of God's Word, not in light of our personal idiosyncrasies and convictions. Only God can judge people's intentions and their hearts. We are on theologically thin and dangerous ice when we try to judge the hearts and intent of others.

Here is an example of how we can damage God's plan with personal judgments against others. I attended a church in the Dallas area that was thriving and growing at a breathtaking pace. The church registered growth in eighteen consecutive months. This growth was achieved even though the church met in a decidedly unattractive former furniture store at a nondescript strip mall. God's blessings seemed to be overflowing.

Then a self-appointed jury decided that the pastor was not the man to lead this church into the future. (I guess they deemed that eighteen-month growth streak just a fluke.) The preacher was judged to be a little too "country," and one church leader even had the chutzpa to tell this pastor that he could see him "pastoring a little church out in East Texas." The audacity of that statement angers me on so many levels. For starters, is God's ministry in small churches somehow less important? Is only a particular type of person suited for God's ministry in the city? At what point did this man become a prophet speaking for how God would use His people? A little glance at the Bible and you just might see that God doesn't always choose the conventional path or person. At any rate, our Church Court, as I called it, found the pastor guilty of "lack of yuppie appeal," and he was essentially forced out of the church.

It gives me no joy to report that the church withered and nearly died. And that little ol' country preacher who was forced out? Today he pastors a healthy and growing church in one of America's largest cities. He has authored seventeen books. God has richly blessed his ministry.

This pastor's case shows a classic example of bad Christians happening to good people. Obviously God blessed the faithfulness of this good man. But who can say what might have happened at that furniture storefront if the Church Court had not forced its way? Based on results, you would be hard pressed to argue that their actions were part of God's will.

By the way, that pastor who was run off was the man who welcomed Katie and our family into his church after we had been rejected and wounded by our previous church family. He made sure Katie was taken care of and that his nursery workers were informed and sensitive to her and to us. Who knows when and even if our family would have returned to a local church had we been rejected again? For that act of Christ's love I will always be grateful to him.

In order for our walkin' to start matchin' our talkin,' the plan is simple—but far from easy.

Prayerfully and honestly evaluate your own life. Then, and only then, can you evaluate the actions of others (not their intent, heart, or salvation). Expect and encourage the best from other Christians. It is worth the effort, 'cause when our walkin' starts matchin' our talkin,' others will start flockin' to the gospel of Christ.

Chapter 7

CSL: Christian As a Second Language

Is sloppiness in speech caused by ignorance or apathy? I don't know and I don't care.

—WILLIAM SAFIRE

Recently I drove by a local church. I'm sure some truly fine, sincere people attend it. I am sure they want to proclaim the truth. I am sure they want to make a difference in the world. On their sign in front of the church were these words:

WE PREACH CHRIST CRUCIFIED

I understood. I speak Christian as a second language. I knew the doctrine of this church by reading that sign. I knew their theological position on salvation and the identity of Christ. But consider the poor folks who are not fluent in Christianese. What goes through their minds? *What the heck does this mean? Do they condone crucifixion?* Frankly, "preaching Christ crucified" sounds a little creepy.

SAY WHAT?

When I travel, one of the things I enjoy is listening to the languages of different people. And I mean just English-speaking people. Every profession from architecture to zookeeping has its own vernacular. Even golfers speak their own language. Have you ever listened to a golfer recount how he hit one fat but laid up to salvage a bogey? Golfers know exactly what that means.

Professionals in my wife's vocation (education) might hear the following exchange:

> **Teacher 1:** Are the SPED students receiving FAPE through ADA and IDEA?
>
> **Teacher 2:** After their CIA is completed and EYS is determined, we will develop an IEP to ensure LRE.
>
> **Teacher 1** *(not even glassy-eyed yet):* Most of the students in CM/CBSE are HI, OI, LD, ED, PDD, or SI.
>
> **Teacher 2** *(rising to the challenge):* In our elementary schools we offer ECI in the PIP or PAT programs.
>
> **Teacher 1** *(I see your abbreviation and I raise you):* Plus there is PPCD, or they can be mainstreamed with HT support or receive CM, CBSE, LIFE, or BA.

You get the idea. By the way, if you are interested, here is the translation for the above conversation.

Teacher 1: Are the **SP**ecial **ED**ucation students receiving **F**ree **A**ppropriate **P**ublic **E**ducation through the **A**mericans with **D**isabilities **A**ct and the **I**ndividuals with **D**isabilities **E**ducation **A**ct?

Teacher 2: After their **C**omprehensive **I**ndividual **A**ssessment is completed and the **E**xtended **Y**ear **S**ervice is determined, we will develop an **I**ndividual **E**ducational **P**rogram to ensure the **L**east **R**estrictive **E**nvironment.

Teacher 1: Most of the students in **C**ontent **M**astery or **C**ampus **B**ased **S**pecial **E**ducation are **H**ealth **I**mpaired, **O**rthopedically **I**mpaired, **L**earning **D**isabled, **E**motionally **D**isturbed, have **P**ervasive **D**evelopment **D**isorder, or are **S**peech **I**mpaired.

Teacher 2: In our elementary schools we offer **E**arly **C**hildhood **I**ntervention in the **P**arents **I**n **P**artnership or **P**arents **A**s **T**eachers programs.

Teacher 1: Plus there is a **P**reschool **P**rogram for **C**hildren with **D**isabilities, or they can be mainstreamed with **H**elping **T**eachers support or receive **C**ontent **M**astery, **C**ampus **B**ased **S**pecial

Education, **L**earning **I**n a **F**unctional **E**nvironment,
or **B**ehavior **A**djustment.

When Christians speak to one another, and even to nonbelievers, we often speak in our own code as well. Phrases that mean
something to the Christian are often confusing or simply bizarre to
a person unfamiliar with the faith.

Christian: "Brother, are you saved?"

Target: "Huh?"

Christian: "Have you been washed in the precious
blood of Jesus?"

Target: "Excuse me?"

Christian: "Don't you know you are a sinner
doomed to the devil's fiery pit of hell?"

Target: "You have a nice day too."

Granted, this exchange is a bit exaggerated, but I have witnessed (and in fact been the target of) several bewildering dia-
logues like this.

I remember sitting in church services as a hormonally raging
teenager trying desperately to live a good Christian life. At the
little church I attended in Chillicothe, Ohio, one particular old
saint would always stand and proclaim that she was saved, sancti-

fied, and loosed from the devil's ways. I would sit there and think, "Sure, you are too old to be interested in the devil's ways. But I'm sitting here next to Betty Jane" (name changed to protect my marriage).

As I have gotten older I have come to understand what she was saying (kind of), but I wonder how often we offend, confuse, and repel the unchurched with our secret language and, in particular, our language of condemnation and fear (see chapter 4). On yet another church kiosk that I passed was the title of the coming Sunday's sermon: The Mortification of the Flesh. That should bring them flocking in! To the non-Christian, this kind of mortification probably sounds like something that might require an amputation.

The gospel is actually very simple when it is spoken clearly. God loves us, but our human nature has separated us from Him. We must find a way to bridge the gap. Our bridge is Jesus Christ, who paid the highest price to redeem us. In God's plan to reach out to us, Christ took our place and suffered the punishment that we should have to pay. Jesus' sacrificial death provided a way for humans to be accepted in the presence of a Holy God. We are offered that gift of salvation (reconciliation to God) by simply believing that Jesus died in our place. There is nothing we can do to earn our way into His presence. Salvation is gained by the grace (an undeserved favor and blessing) of God. Period.

And yet we have confused the simple good news of the gospel with as much gobbledygook as those legal disclaimers at the end of television car commercials. Consider the column I found in the religious section of the *Dallas Morning News* prior to Easter (2000). The article opened with this: "Christians believe, teach, and confess that a new covenant between God, the Holy Trinity, and the human race was created by the sacrificial, shed blood of Jesus Christ, the Incarnate Son and Second Person of the Trinity, at Golgotha on Good Friday." Uhhhh. Okay.

Christianity can easily become cliché-anity when we drop phrases like these:

"I have Jesus in my heart."

"Jesus died for me."

"I am a Spirit-filled believer."

"Are you saved?"

We throw out words and phrases that sound spiritual. We assume that listeners know what these words mean and, more critically, what the words mean for them. Sadly, we Christians often don't even know what they mean to us. Every person who wishes to explain his faith in Jesus Christ to nonbelievers must take the time to gain a working knowledge of the faith and the ability to clearly explain theological terms.

Now, I acknowledge that understanding the theological basis of our beliefs can be difficult. Some things about the faith can't be easily explained. After all, that's what makes it a walk of faith. But the majority of what we believe should be as clear to us as other important aspects of our lives. We take the time to learn about our investments. Yet it is far easier to say *sanctification* or *justification* than it is to understand and explain the meaning of either one. We can explain capital gains, but not Communion; treasury notes but not the Trinity. We take the time to learn sports terms. I can explain a nickel defense in football more easily than I can detail the New Covenant. I can name every professional sports team, but not all the books of the Old Testament. That is to my shame. Further, I have observed that if I cannot explain what a particular theological term means, it is a very real possibility that I have not fully incorporated it into my own life.

As with most aspects of the faith, clarifying our language calls for balance. I am not advocating "dumbing" down our faith to communicate to the masses. I am not advocating translating our beliefs into a vapid touchy-feely spiritual psychobabble. (There are five words I never dreamed I would string together.) If we were to swing the pendulum too far in the other direction, the result would be meaningless tripe not unlike this politically correct greeting that made the Internet rounds last year:

> Please accept—with no obligation, implied or
> implicit—our best wishes for an environmentally
> conscious, socially responsible, low stress, nonaddic-
> tive, gender neutral, celebration of the winter sol-
> stice holiday, practiced within the most enjoyable
> traditions of the religious persuasion of your choice,
> or secular practices of your choice, with respect for
> the religious/secular persuasions and/or traditions of
> others, or their choice not to practice religious or
> secular traditions at all…and a fiscally successful,
> personally fulfilling, and medically uncomplicated
> recognition of the onset of the generally accepted
> calendar year 2001, but not without due respect for
> the calendars of choice of other cultures whose con-
> tributions to society have helped make America

great (not to imply that America is necessarily greater than any other country or is the only "America" in the western hemisphere), and without regard to the race, creed, color, age, physical ability, religious faith, choice of computer platform, or sexual preference of the wishee. (By accepting this greeting, you are accepting these terms. This greeting is subject to clarification or withdrawal. It is freely transferable with no alteration to the original greeting. It implies no promise by the wisher to actually implement any of the wishes for her/himself or others, and is void where prohibited by law, and is revocable at the sole discretion of the wisher. This wish is warranted to perform as expected within the usual application of good tidings for a period of one year, or until the issuance of a subsequent holiday greeting, whichever comes first, and warranty is limited to replacement of this wish or issuance of a new wish at the sole discretion of the wisher.)

If only we could hire interpreters to accompany many of the brethren as they talk about their belief in Christ. Here is a sample translation.

> "Brother, are you saved?"
> *Have you heard the incredible news that you can have a personal relationship with God?*

"You are a sinner in the eyes of God."
Everyone falls short of the perfect nature of a Holy
God. It is impossible for anyone to live a life that
would please God. All sin is the same in God's eyes,
and it really doesn't matter how good a life we live.
Sin still separates us from a Holy God.

"Without Jesus you will be doomed to the fiery
pit of hell."
God loved you so much that He became a man. He
came to earth in the person of Jesus and experienced
life as we do. Then He let men kill Him. He died in
our place so we wouldn't have to be punished with
eternal death for the things we have done wrong.
Then He rose from the dead, and because He now
lives, we have a way for you to avoid eternal separa-
tion from Him.

"You must be washed in the blood of Jesus."
Jesus was wrongly killed, but even that tragedy was
part of God's plan. You see, Jesus took our sin on
Himself by dying, and then He conquered sin and
death by coming to life again. When we accept this
loving sacrifice that He made for us, we can experience
God's deep and abiding love for us on a daily basis.

When speaking to your non-Christian friends and family members, it is possible to hit the mark where truth and comprehension

intersect. Pray for the ability to hit that mark more often than not. The challenge to Christians (present company included) is simple: Know what you believe (more on that important topic in chapter 13). Be able to explain it clearly in plain English, custom tailored to your audience. Who knows, you might learn something in the process.

Chapter 8

Godly or Gaudy?

Nobody ever went broke underestimating the taste of the American public.

—H. L. MENCKEN

Last night I had a dream. I went shopping with Jesus. We were browsing through a Christian book superstore. He stopped at the What Would Jesus Do? bracelet display. I found out what Jesus would do. He moved on. Jesus picked up the Testamints breath mints and examined them. Next he saw the Jesus and His dog statue portraying a young Jesus with a German shepherd. Did I see Him chuckle? The Jesus Saves air freshener for cars caught His attention. He looked around at the rows of products and aisles of books, row after row of books about Jesus and how to know Him and be like Him and so on and so on. "Why do you make faith so complicated?" He asked quietly. "I didn't say figure Me out. I said follow Me." That woke me up.

I am not opposed to making money. As unlikely as the scenario is, I wouldn't mind making money from this book. But I can't help but wonder if all the "Christian" products send the right message. I know this is where my cynicism meter peaks. And try as I might I have been unable to determine anywhere in the Bible where cynicism is a spiritual gift. But I do have some concerns about the marketing of Jesus.

GET A LOAD OF THIS!

I was okay with the WWJD bracelets. I liked the idea of the subtle yet visible reminder of the reality of a daily relationship with Christ. My wedding band is a similar reality check. My ring has intertwined gold bands to symbolize our marriage and four small diamonds to remind me of my children. Three healthy sons are a daily part of my life. The fourth diamond represents the short but meaningful life of our daughter, Katie. When things go south, I have trained myself to look at that band and get things in perspective. Rarely is something more important than what that wedding band represents. And that refocusing helps bring me back to my spiritual foundation in Christ.

Given the value of reality reminders in my own life, the WWJD craze seemed harmless enough. However, by the time we got to WWJD boxer shorts complete with false fly, I had reached the saturation point. Somehow the idea of dropping trou to be reminded of what Jesus would do seemed to have veered slightly away from the original concept.

Speaking of a fly (he transitioned smoothly), how about the Gospel Fly for bringing your unchurched, unsaved friends to the faith? The Gospel Fly is a fishing fly to be worn on your lapel that will make you a fisher of men. When your friend asks you what kind of fly that is on your lapel (which would happen to me constantly), you are instructed to reply, "This isn't a fly for fish. It's a fly for making me a fisher of men." Or an optional gender modification for women is to call it a *people fly*. Oh, by the way, in the suggested script your nosy friend is referred to as a fish. Follow the script, hook your perspective fish, and add him to your eternal stringer. Remember to put on your WWJD waders—and good fishing!

You no doubt thought I was kidding with the "Jesus Saves" air freshener. It actually did exist in a convenient three-pack, and the back packaging encouraged you to spread the word: "Express your feelings with this beautiful, meaningful air freshener. Use it anywhere…wherever a pleasant aroma is desired or an odor problem exists." I must ask: Can air freshener really be meaningful?

At a recent Christian trade show I encountered a mind-boggling array of "Christian" stuff. Want the scent of salvation? We now have Christian cologne. Thought about wearing a fish cross Christian toe ring for witnessing during your pedicure? You got it.

I was thrilled to find out that my SUV can now take over my evangelistic responsibilities entirely. Of course I will have the standard fish cross on the rear bumper. Next to that I can cover my infidel spare tire with a "Jesus Loves You" genuine vinyl tire cover. In the window I will display my "Jesus on Board" sign, which at least ought to get me a better parking place at church. On those hot Texas days a Christian sunshade will reach the multitudes at the mall. Thieves will retreat when they see my "Warning…This Property Protected by Jesus" sticker. On the front bumper my tasteful "Don't wait for the hearse to take you to church" license tag will turn some folks around. And finally, for speed-readers on the roadways, I can affix this bumper sticker: "Practice safe sex...get married and be faithful (or just abstain)... God says so... Ephesians 5:3 & 1 Corinthians 7:1-4." The references may be tough to note at seventy miles per hour, but it's the message that counts.

For Christian athletes, the Sports Angels pin will add that little extra edge that your unchurched competition won't be able to match. For example, the Guardian Golf Angel is crafted in a gold and silver antique finish with the angel in a full backswing (nearly hitting its wings). The brochure says the angel will watch over your drives and putts. Apparently even angels struggle with their short game. A photo of a frustrated golfer trying to blast out of the bunker is accompanied by the caption, "She forgot to wear her golf angel." I'm thinking my golf angel may have a need for earplugs in the event that he fails to "watch over" certain fairway shots.

Another amazing way to win converts at work is the Almighty Pager. For only five dollars a month you can receive pages with Bible verses. According to the company, "By receiving pages from God you will not only learn the Bible, but you will be able to share the messages with others." No kidding. "Excuse me, boys," you say loudly. "I'd better take this one." Dramatic pause. "It's from God." That should get you some attention at the old staff meeting. God beeps in mysterious ways His wonders to perform.

Perhaps my favorite on the Velvet Elvis scale of great tackiness is the Mother Teresa singing doll. In authentic headpiece and habit, this key-wind musical doll sings (and I'm not kidding) "You Light Up My Life." Perhaps next we can get a Pope John doll crooning "Candle in the Wind." There really is no end to the possibilities.

After you've enjoyed the Mother Teresa cover of Debbie Boone, I recommend trying to assemble the Keys to Death and Hell jigsaw puzzle. For the sake of your eternity, try not to lose any pieces.

If you can't go to where Moses walked, you can now walk on the soil he trod...every day! The Holy Steps insoles are filled with holy soil from Jerusalem on the bottom layer. The middle layer absorbs perspiration to minimize the need to add a "Jesus Saves" air freshener to your closet.

If you wish your footwear to be a little more, well, evangelistic, you will drool over the Shoes of the Fisherman sandals. They are imprinted with *Jesus* on the left sole and *Loves You* on the right. According to the marketers you can leave a message "in the sand at the seashore, on sidewalks after a rain shower, and on wet pool decks." This sole-to-soul outreach is truly unique.

If you have a brother who backslides a bit or perhaps is Episcopalian, the Twelve Apostles Beer Mug makes a thoughtful gift. A toast to Peter, Luke, and all the gang will be a spiritual experience unlike any other. Twelve apostles, twelve pack. Coincidence?

Looking for opportunities to sneak a little prayer time into your busy life? Look no further. The fine folks at JMJ Products have devised a plastic-coated prayer card to hang in the shower. "What better way to start your day than to say the Morning Offering while lathering up?" they ask. You could also meditate on Scripture, I suppose. How about "and they realized they were naked"?

I am all for presenting the image of Jesus as love and God as our Father. But a T-shirt from Sonrise Christian Wear made me a little uncomfortable with its casual familiarity. On the back of the shirt is a note pinned to a cross with this message.

> Gone to see Dad.
> We're fixin' a place for you.
> Be back soon to pick you up.
>
> Jesus

Fixin' a place? Is it in Texas? Somehow the majesty of "Be still and know that I am Dad" just isn't the same.

Finishing strong, I present Jesus the Hot Air Balloon. This gigantic hot air balloon toured the U.S. with its message "King of Kings, Lord of Lords" across the back. Merritt Ministry faced head on the challenge of "How do you create a hot air balloon that is both authentic and reverent in its mission of communicating Jesus, the Son of God?" A daunting task for anyone. Jesus the Hot Air Balloon weighs over 750 pounds and is filled with 258,000 cubits…er…cubic feet of air. He is 110 feet tall. (Wait a minute! Did Jesus the Hot Air Balloon happen to be in Tulsa when Oral Roberts was getting his hospital vision? Just wondering.)

PRODUCTS OR PRINCIPLES?

Sometimes it seems that we try a little too hard to make everything "Christian." What's next? Will we be marketing Christian chairs or Christian computers? I hope that instead we follow the example of men like S. Truett Cathy, the founder of Chick-Fil-A. He runs a company that clearly has a Christian focus and makes a remarkable statement in today's culture by closing on Sundays. But what has made Chick-Fil-A successful? Is it the testimony of Mr. Cathy? Is it the day of rest designated for employees to worship? I would humbly suggest that the reason is great tasting chicken. That is why I became a patron. In fact, I was well aware of the great chicken long before I learned the rest of the Chick-Fil-A story. Now I feel even better about patronizing this company because I know that this corporation models integrity and that a portion of the profits goes to support ministries. Mr. Cathy has a particular heart for children needing foster homes, and his company contributes hundreds of thousands of dollars annually to foster homes in the southeast. Doesn't that make you feel just a little better when you order that chicken sandwich and a little less guilty when you add dessert? But I still would not go there if the chicken didn't taste great.

There are many examples of companies who make great products and happen to have Christian values. Norm Miller is the president of Interstate Batteries in Dallas. They make a great product and have a wonderful company that is active in ministries around the world. But they don't make "Christian" batteries. They are a company that makes good batteries and operates according to solid Christian principles. Premier Design Jewelry is a direct sales company founded by a dynamic and visionary Christian couple, Andy and Joan Horner. From their profits, they give money to missionaries all over the world. They do not sell "Christian" jewelry. They sell beautiful jewelry, and their company worldview demands integrity in the marketplace. The integration of quality without ethical compromise will get the attention of at least some consumers.

I am a coffee-aholic. If the Betty Ford Center built the Juan Valdez Java Wing, I would be a prime candidate. For many years I gave my coffee dollars (and lots of them) to a large company that is now located in every zip code except for one or two in Alaska and North Dakota. Then I came across a company with a Christian worldview. It's called Pura Vida Coffee (http://www.puravidacoffee. com). They buy from co-ops that support family farms in Costa Rica. They then give 100 percent of their net profits to children and families in Costa Rica and Central America. They don't send me "Christian" coffee beans. They send me wonderful coffee perfectly roasted. It is delicious, one of the finest coffees I have discovered. And while I am enjoying Pura Vida Coffee, I love the thought that some of my purchase helps minister to kids in Costa Rica.

As more companies like this come to the forefront, we can get out of the boycott mentality and into the compassionate Christian consumer category. We are a factor in the marketplace. *U.S. News and World Report* noted that the income of Christian adults was one trillion dollars in 1995. One way to have a cultural impact is by what we do (support companies like these) and what we don't do. As you have probably figured out by now, I am not a big supporter of noisy boycotts. They tend to merely promote free of charge whatever we detest. A good example of this mentality is the recent debut of the unbelievably tacky *Temptation Island* on Fox Network. This show (on its merits) did not deserve a moment of consideration from Christians, people with kids, or anyone smarter than a Chihuahua. Yet here we come with the public outcries, adding bushels of forbidden fruit to this tasteless tripe. I would venture a guess that the marketing executives count on Christian condemnation as a huge part of their marketing strategy.

Since the Garden of Eden, human beings have been drawn to the forbidden. When we loudly condemn what's prohibited, our strategy generally backfires, and we end up amplifying the attraction. Instead, why don't we use our influence (we have the numbers, after all) to make a positive impact for companies showing integrity and compassion in the marketplace? I realize that identifying those companies can be a challenge. Several mutual funds invest in just such companies, and finding a list of their investment choices would be a good start. We can't spend every dollar with such companies, but identifying and supporting those corporations that operate according to Judeo-Christian principles would be an important step.

And if you can help further various ministries by purchasing things that you already are planning to buy…isn't that a no-brainer? An Internet shopping site called KingdomBuy.com allows a percentage of every purchase you make online to be rebated to a ministry or church that you designate. No extra cost. Just a little more money coming back to the Lord's work. We need to maximize every angle as Christian consumers and use our combined power to quietly make a difference. I am anxious for more companies with a Christian worldview to step forward so that we can support them with our consumer power. A reverse boycott, if you will.

Supporting the positive is so much more uplifting and fulfilling.

Finally, I didn't mean to come off as a total jerk about some of the products mentioned earlier. I would just like to see an emphasis on great work and quality products that just happen to be made by Christians.

Oh, there is one more item that I left for last. Finally, and I do mean finally, you will definitely want the Talking Tombstone. I plan on spending $4,995 on this motion-detecting memorial that will scare the bejeebers out of anyone passing by my final resting place. A recorded message will blast out anytime the beam is broken. I already have recorded my message:

> Hi! This is—I mean was—Dave. I'm truly sorry if you thought any of these products were great ideas. I apologize if I offended you. If you are here to sue the estate, the kids have already spent it. Have a nice eternity. If you need further assistance, check your Almighty Pager.

Chapter 9

Jesus Wept...
and He Still Does

The Anti-Defamation League lists nearly 5,000 hate sites on the Internet. According to their research about 300 of those use Bible verses or church language to promote their cause.

—SOUTHERN LEGAL RESEARCH INSTITUTE

If you have read this far, you have no doubt surmised I was a smart-aleck kid. When my Sunday-school teachers used to give candy for memorizing a Bible verse, I would roll in on Sunday morning (at least the first time) and brightly proclaim: "John 11:35. 'Jesus wept.'"

The shortest verse in the Bible. Look it up. Interestingly, that verse still comes to mind every time I am saddened by tragic news. And I can't help but think that verse applied when Jesus witnessed the appalling reaction by some who claimed to be His followers to one particularly tragic and senseless death in 1998.

I will never forget the pain that pierced my heart when I turned on the evening news. A young gay man named Matthew

Shepard had been cruelly beaten to death in Wyoming by two cowardly thugs. Then my pain turned to revulsion. At his funeral in Wyoming, a man waved a sign bearing Matthew's face and the words, "Matt is in hell." I grieved for Matthew's family and friends. I prayed that somehow God would help them to realize that the sign did not represent how Christ or His sincere followers felt about the young man's death. I agonized for the group of hate-filled people who had so entirely missed Jesus that they could invoke His name so outrageously. And I felt additionally sick that the faith that sustains me had been misrepresented and broadly displayed in this way.

Fred Phelps, the so-called pastor from Kansas who promotes his "God Hates Fags" Web site, somehow managed to become the media-appointed spokesperson on Matthew's death for conservative Christianity. I tried to go to Phelps's Web site to see what he had to say in a context broader than a sound bite. One must question how much glory a ministry gives to God's kingdom when Christian software filters censor its Web site for hateful rhetoric. I imagine Phelps would just chalk up the censorship to the prevalent failure among Christians to see "truth" as he does. Thank God that few do. I was going to cite some examples from his Web page, but his position is too disgusting to repeat.

When such despicable behavior becomes the public perception of Christian response, even the most thoughtful and caring protests against the gay lifestyle become labeled "hateful" and "bigoted." If the average gay or lesbian thinks I break bread with Fred Phelps, I can understand that fear and even loathing. (By the way, my omission of the title Reverend from Phelps's name is deliberate.

My dictionary defines *reverend* as being "worthy of reverence or entitled to respect." In my opinion Phelps is 0 for 2.)

Some groups blame conservative Christians for Matthew Shepard's death. They link fundamentalists to "homophobic" attitudes that created an environment conducive to the killing. I would be the first to admit that the church (yes, that includes me) has done a miserable job overall of understanding and ministering to those who embrace a gay lifestyle. But when we are accused of creating a scenario in which faith is liable for a cowardly act of hate, I have to dissent. Evil is evil. These killers were evil. They acted out of hate.

It's been noted that the Bible states six admonishments to homosexuals. There are well over three hundred directed toward heterosexuals. Let's be honest: We straight believers have a vast, toxic superfund cleanup in our own backyards as well.

Some Christian groups will call me a gay sympathizer. They will call me a lover of people of color. Actually, they will call me much worse, but you get the point. They will call me a Jew supporter. They will be right on every charge. I have no choice. For when God created man in His image, He made no mention of color, race, education, income, or any other qualifier. You can rest assured that I want to be standing firmly in the corner of God's chosen people.

When the Bible proclaims that whosoever believes shall have eternal life, that means everyone. God's grace is not exclusively for the rich, pretty, smart, or talented. God's grace is available to everyone. God's plan of salvation is in fact the great leveler of the human playing field. Donald Trump comes to his eternal destiny with the same assets or lack thereof as you or I will. I like the thought that Mr. Trump will need to wait his turn just like everyone else.

We discussed earlier how all of those who use the name *Christian* are often lumped together by non-Christians. While it is tough enough to get blamed for your own mistakes, it is really frustrating to be indicted for those who share your title but not your convictions. Those claiming the name of Christ have tolerated and even initiated hateful messages (and I'm not sure which is worse), and this troubles me greatly. I have always been sympathetic to police departments whenever an incident implicates an officer in illegal or unethical behavior. I am sure that an overwhelming percentage of policemen and women are professional and caring. I thank God they are willing to serve and protect us. But when one rogue cop dominates the headlines, the entire profession is judged to be guilty by association. It is a sad twist of our human nature that a rogue element of less than 1 percent can ruin the public perception of the remaining 99. Likewise, the church has had (and still does have) rogue representatives of Christ.

THE HISTORY WORKING AGAINST US

If you have engaged unbelievers in substantive discussions about Christianity, you have no doubt been pummeled with a litany of atrocities committed in the name of Christ. The Inquisition. Slavery. Acceptance of Jim Crow laws. Degradation of women. Hatred of homosexuals. Persecution of Jews. And the charges are true. All are to the shame of the church. We should have known better, and if we did know better, we should have done something. Our lack of discernment, dearth of personal knowledge of God's Word, and lack of moral courage allowed such sin to exist for decades and even centuries. It is a fact that the church has committed egregious sins in alleged service of the Lord.

I would certainly argue that these sins were the result of men and women acting entirely outside of the will of God and in direct opposition to Christ's teachings. While a just God will judge fairly, Christianity has too often wrongly taken it upon itself to judge and condemn those who don't believe. In our zeal for evangelism, we have historically sinned against other cultures, races, and creeds. There is no biblical basis for the brutal tactics of some; no support for these acts can be found in Jesus' ministry on earth or in the New Testament. Such methods run contrary to and obliterate both the message of salvation and the loving service of those who follow Christ's teachings more closely.

It is unfortunate that today's critics see the church as the greatest threat to cultural diversity and tolerance. A survey of academics conducted by the Williamsburg Charter Survey on Religion found that one-third of the surveyed university faculty professors consider evangelical Christians a "threat to democracy"! I cringe when I read numbers like that, and my first reaction is defensiveness and anger. But there is painful truth in the criticisms directed at Christians. Corporately, we have earned many of their rebukes through our prideful misrepresentation of Jesus' message for the sake of our own personal agendas.

We have grieved our Lord and given ammunition to those who are skeptical of Christianity. The prophet Nathan confronted

David after his sexual sin with Bathsheba and the subsequently arranged murder of her husband, Uriah. But the prophet's message resonates to every person who claims to represent God. When Nathan admonished David, he said, "By doing this you have made the enemies of the LORD show utter contempt" (2 Samuel 12:14). God forbid that we do any more to give skeptics and seekers cause to show utter contempt toward the faith.

When I was growing up, I regularly heard comments like this from former Georgia Governor Lester Maddox: "Why would we have different races if God meant us to be alike and associate with each other?" Such statements generally went unchallenged by the Christian church. The church is like Wall Street. We don't like uncertainty. Jumping into the middle of the racial debate would have made us a little jittery, so we effectively decided to pass until the civil rights movement made it impossible to ignore. We (the church) should have led that charge much sooner.

In 1990 my beloved Cincinnati Reds unexpectedly went to the World Series. I endeared myself to my wonderful wife by purchasing World Series tickets even though we were living in Texas and were a little tight on money. Priorities, you know. I was sitting in the upper deck at what was then Riverfront Stadium (now Cinergy Field) with the Reds taking on the highly favored Oakland As. In this particular game the Reds' brilliant shortstop, Barry Larkin, made a spectacular play to save an exciting Reds win. As MC Hammer's music blared, I began celebrating wildly. I high-fived and hugged all the Reds fans around me, all of them total strangers. I found myself hugging a black Reds fan and jumping up and down with him.

Later I reflected on that. Would I have been as comfortable

hugging him on a public street? Honestly? Probably not. So what was the difference in Riverfront? We experienced the common bond of baseball. I was red and he was red, and that was all that mattered. And then it hit me. Was I as comfortable with my black brothers who are Christians as I was with the black Reds fan? If the bond of sports brought us together, how can the bond of faith not unite races even more? Sadly, the greatest progress in the area of racial reconciliation seems in fact to be taking place at sporting events, not at church.

PREVENTING DÉJÀ VU

Recently I came across a disturbing book called *Without Sanctuary.* It details the tragic history of mob lynching in America. The photos are chilling, disgusting, and heartbreaking. But perhaps the most disturbing photos are the images captured after the deaths. People had their pictures taken with the victims like hunting trophies. Leonard Pitts, a columnist from Miami, once came across an old newspaper headline that unbelievably stated, "A good time is had by all as Negro is put to death."

Why am I dredging up the past? You might be thinking, "That doesn't happen anymore." My question is this: How could the church stand aside and allow this to happen? If we don't know the answer, our chances of keeping history from repeating itself are slim to none. I can somewhat safely say that such atrocities won't happen again in such a grotesquely public way, but the evil that generated those brutalities still exists in the hearts of men. For years I personally dodged the issue by assuring myself that I could never do such a thing. I probably am right about that. But a statement from author Elie Weisel haunts me as I consider the state of our culture. He says, "The opposite of love, I have found, is not hate, but indifference."

Ouch. Talk about shattering my comfortable little rationalizations. Even if I have not hated to such a degree, I have been indifferent. And the indifference of the church and Christians is the hole in the fence that allows evil to crawl through unencumbered.

Recently I read a 1933 interview with Adolf Hitler. The strategies that would nearly destroy the world were clearly in place at this time. Even Hitler realized that the Jewish heritage of Jesus could not be challenged.

"You cannot make Jesus an Aryan. That is rubbish," he stated. And yet Hitler's strategy to destroy the church is chilling, and I will reproduce that portion of the interview in its rambling but devastating entirety. The emphasis is my own.

> The Catholic Church is already something great.
> Good God, people, this is an institution, and it has
> already had a two-thousand-year existence. We
> must learn from it. It is instilled with wisdom and
> human understanding. They know their people!
> They know what people are all about. But now
> their time is up! The priests themselves know this.
> They are smart enough; they realize this and do not
> engage in a fight. If they should, I will certainly not
> make martyrs out of them. *We will brand them as
> simple criminals. I will rip the mask of respectability
> from their faces. And if that is not enough. I will make*

them laughable and contemptuous. I will have movies written. We will show the history of the priests in film. The people can be amazed at the whole mess of nonsense, selfishness, stupidity, and fraud. How they stole money from the peasantry. How they tried to outdo the Jews. How they committed incest. We will make it so exciting that everyone will want to see it. The people will stand in lines outside the theaters. And if the hair of the pious citizens should stand on their necks, so much the better. The youth will understand it. The youth and the people. I will gladly give up the others. I guarantee...if I want I could destroy the Church in a few years. It is all so hollow and the whole belief system is fragile and untruthful through and through. When pushed with a little force it will collapse. With their demonstrated desire for profit and good living, we will easily get them. On that point we can be of one accord. I give them a couple of years' reprieve. Why do we need to argue? *They will swallow everything in order to maintain their material position. It won't come to a fight.*

(Dokumente zur Kirchenpolitik des 3 Reiches, Band 1, Das Jahr 1933. Translated by David Crabtree, professor at Gutenberg College, Eugene, Oregon, *Context*, April 1998.)

Hitler's concepts stunned and sobered me. You will notice that he never challenged Christ. His focus was the church. And his strategy was to make them laughable. A joke. Fools. He would use the entertainment medium of films to plant the message he wanted to communicate. His target was the young and the disenfranchised. He conceded that a few faithful would be impossible to persuade, and he wouldn't waste his time with them. The rest were easy; those people were his target. Draw whatever parallels you wish to our current society. Hitler was smart enough not to make martyrs of the believers. He planned to defeat the church leaders by threatening their material possessions, not their theology. And he accomplished his task without spreading untruths about the church. Sadly, the plan worked pretty well. And it created an environment that allowed the Holocaust to happen with minimal opposition from the church.

I have read Hitler's comments repeatedly since first discovering them. Would I have been so easily swayed? Worse yet, am I being that easily swayed by today's culture? Perhaps I should prayerfully examine whether I am being influenced by the "comfortable" state of the church in America. Winston Churchill noted, "We are stripped bare by the curse of plenty." I fear that the church and modern Christians have become increasingly willing, as Hitler said, to swallow anything to maintain our material position.

Believers' faith in the *church* paved the way for Hitler's near success with this strategy. Faith in *Christ* would not have allowed it. God help us to see the difference.

Chapter 10

The Culture War: Rambo or Conscientious Objector?

When you don't know what to do, walk fast and look worried.

—DILBERT'S RULES OF ORDER

Given the tension the culture war creates among Christians, Dilbert's plan might be as good as any. *The culture war* has become a catchall phrase for the age-old question of how believers fit into and engage popular culture. The word *war* in this phrase is revealing: *Many Christians view much of popular culture and the people in it as mortal enemies.*

War or not, many bright and well-intentioned believers have different ideas about exactly what is the "correct" strategy for engaging the culture. The Rambo sector charges in with all weapons blazing at every real or perceived threat to religious freedom. Some of us are conscientious objectors; we wear love beads and sing "Give

Peace a Chance" while we disengage from society and hang out at church potlucks and Bunco parties. Some of us choose the approach my sons take when it comes to mowing and watering our lawn: If we ignore it long enough, perhaps the problems will just die out.

Still others decide to let the "professional" Christians handle this battle while we pray for them at a considerable distance from the front lines. This spiritual strategy is not unlike the military approach exposed by a fascinating article in the May 15, 2000, issue of *Newsweek* titled "The Kosovo Cover-Up." The Clinton administration, according to *Newsweek,* had authorized a risk-free war strategy in the Balkan wars. The United States wanted to be involved, but not at the risk of American lives, so instead we sent money and air power to cripple the Serbian strongman Slobodan Milosevic. The idea was to strategically attack targets from high altitudes with smart bombs.

Reporters John Barry and Evan Thomas detailed the real story about what was initially proclaimed the "most successful air campaign ever." General Henry Shelton had joined Defense Secretary William Cohen to declare the destruction of Milosevic's firepower as initial reports indicated that more than half of the artillery and one-third of the armored vehicles were destroyed. The numbers were incredible. NATO's forces had killed 120 tanks, roughly 220 armored personnel carriers, and up to 450 artillery and mortar pieces. The conclusion we drew was exciting: We could now fight wars with minimal risk to our troops.

But the truth gradually leaked out, and *Newsweek* detailed the actual results. There were only 14 confirmed tank kills, not 120, and only 18 armored personnel carriers taken out, not 220. The

450 artillery pieces? Only 20 were actually destroyed. The cunning Kosovo forces fashioned decoy targets for the pilots to hit. At thirty-six thousand feet, the artillery decoy of long black logs on old truck wheels looked exactly like the intended targets. We destroyed dozens of decoys and fake bridges and blew up lots of stuff. We put on quite an air show, but it had little impact on Milosevic's power.

I fall into the group of Christians who have adopted such a battle plan. We attempt to "smart bomb" cultural targets with money, boycotts, and political action. We figure that if we can strategically strike targets by sending out parachurch organizations or by helping fund Christian political action groups, we won't get wounded. Personal safety is, after all, our utmost concern. Unfortunately, most Christian smart bombs launched from safe altitudes have generally destroyed decoys, targets that don't matter, or merely provided a spectacular fireworks show. Perhaps the best example of such a strategy was the influx of money into organizations like the Moral Majority in the late 1980s. Cal Thomas has detailed in his book *Blinded by Might* how the religious right invested millions into changing the culture through political power and, in his opinion, failed mightily. Organizations like the Moral Majority did create a lot of fireworks and even took out a target or two, but it would be hard to argue that the culture was significantly improved for the investment of money and time.

In reality, the culture war is neither antiseptic and safe nor bent on Rambo-like destruction. God calls us to be in the trenches doing battle with the issues that really matter.

If we want to be effective, we must first define what we hope to accomplish within our culture and what we can do to achieve those objectives. If I were to ask the average Christian what victory in the culture war would look like today, I would probably get answers along these lines: Abortion would be outlawed. Homosexuality would be suppressed. The Ten Commandments would hang in every courthouse, and kids would pray in school.

But would accomplishing these objectives constitute true victory? During the Gulf War, the United States military demonstrated one of the most decisive military advantages in modern history, and we emerged victorious. I think historians would agree, however, that by leaving Saddam Hussein in power, we fell short of the higher goal.

Most of us think it is our mission as Christians to rid the world of sin. That is not going to happen. We have tried through politics and failed miserably. We have tried boycotts. When I last checked, Disney was still in business. We tried advertising and media with very mixed results. We have targeted immorality but have not helped those hurt by or entrapped in it. We fight abortion. We fear homosexuality. We denounce drugs. We battle Hollywood and television and the evil media. We criticize the music industry and seek to ban records. We rail against pornography.

As a young man who went through middle school and high school in the late '60s and early '70s, I can confirm that all of the aforementioned cultural indicators now sought by many Christians were once in place: There was no legalized abortion or aggressive gay agenda. We prayed at school functions and watched Ozzie and Harriet on television instead of *Sex in the City*. Yet the sexual revolution, recreational drugs, violent political protest, and explosive racial tension emerged from this very era.

We Christians have missed our calling. The church needs to

understand that even if we devoured every single moral issue on our evangelical plates, the people of this world would still be seeking meaning and purpose in their lives. All of the cultural issues I've mentioned so far are merely symptoms of a bigger problem: the internal condition of millions of people. Political and legal processes can only restrain sin. Advertising campaigns or education can, at best, only restrain behavior, and that is not a viable long-term solution. I heard a comment from a college student that illustrates this. "I said no to drugs," he said, "but they just wouldn't listen." Funny. But tragically true. Only the changing of individuals can really affect a society as a whole. And that is where we have missed the boat. We can attempt legislation of morals until the end of time. But change comes from the inside (heart) out...rarely from the outside (rules) in.

It is time for us to add a new dimension to our approach.

For Christians, the battle at the heart of the culture war is between competing worldviews. The Christian worldview holds that there is absolute truth, a clear delineation between right and wrong. Human life is precious. Human beings are inherently sinful, and no amount of social programs or education or external influence will make us good. We have these truths on the authority of God's Word. Other worldviews claim that humans are inherently good and therefore quite capable of building a utopian-like society in which education and knowledge will solve all problems. There is no absolute truth. Instead, truth is an evolving entity subject to change as new information becomes available.

Guess what? Christians have a message that can *change people,* and proclaiming it should be our primary mission. We have a worldview that works. We need to understand it, defend it, and live it.

I confess that determining my personal response as a Christian to my role in the culture war has been an intellectual struggle. Frankly, I have changed positions more frequently than a student with ADHD during a boring lecture. For now, I have reached a couple of conclusions. First is the realization that we believers are in the unique situation of possessing dual citizenship. We are citizens of both earth and of heaven. We have responsibilities in both arenas. As a citizen of the United States, I am responsible for involving myself in the processes of freedom. I need to know the issues, know how government works, know who my elected officials are. (Quick: Who is your U.S. House Representative? Your State Representative?) I have all the responsibilities of being a good citizen, such as paying taxes, serving on juries, voting faithfully, and so on. In tandem with these responsibilities are my duties as a citizen of heaven. I am to love my neighbors, feed the poor, and extend to them the hope and grace of the gospel. If we Christians took both roles equally seriously (and I would venture that few of us do), I'm convinced our effect on culture would be far more profound than it currently is.

SABOTAGE!

I have been reading a book by UC-Berkeley Associate Professor of Linguistics John H. McWhorter called *Losing the Race*. In this controversial book he persuasively builds a case that African Americans often (in his words) "self-sabotage their potential in America."

In Mr. McWhorter's opinion, three critical phenomena in African American culture have hurt the advancement of blacks in the United States:

1. The cult of victimization is a tendency to blame problems on nonexistent or overestimated white racism. I must hasten to add that Mr. McWhorter does not say that racism has been eliminated. His point is that looking for it in every event is self-defeating and that racism is less of an issue than many blacks believe.

2. Separatism is the mind-set that encourages blacks to remove themselves from anything labeled white.

3. Anti-intellectualism is an attitude that subtly but effectively convinces black students that too much interest in academics is tantamount to "acting white."

The veracity of Professor McWhorter's theories about the African American community will be debated for some time. But I would suggest that significant parallels can be drawn between his premises and the Christian population. And I would propose that the same three phenomena affect how Christians view their role in society.

1. Victimization

I have been guilty of succumbing to the cult of victimization. How often do we whine and complain that Christians are the only religious group that truly experiences discrimination? Victimization can (and does) become an obsession, and this idea is easy to support with examples if you're looking for them.

I am especially interested in this aspect of Mr. McWhorter's writings as it applies to Christians because *victim* possesses an interesting dual meaning. *Victim* refers to an unfortunate person who suffers from some adverse circumstance. It also refers to a person who is tricked or swindled. Clearly the Christian community has experienced both. But I would tentatively (and in my full defensive posture) suggest that too often we have been tricked by the Enemy into *feeling* victimized.

Clearly, hostility toward Christianity is a reality. Even so, many of our wounds are self-inflicted. Embracing victimhood is manifested in some or all of the following:

- *Paranoia in America that everyone is out to "get" Christians.* Some folks are. But frankly, most are not really interested or don't understand what we are trying to say or do. We haven't lived lives that are different enough for them to notice. When we do, some will turn their heads for a closer look. Many will not. Those are simply the facts of faith. You will be criticized by some no matter how well you live your life. I can show you Internet postings that find fault with Mother Teresa and Billy Graham. What chance do I have to avoid criticism? Not only that, but we U.S. citizens should be fully aware of and thankful that the worst that we endure in the name of Christ is most often nothing compared to the persecution suffered by many believers around the world.

- *Belief that the media is evil.* The media is secular and will behave like secular media behaves. Christians don't need the media to accomplish what God desires. Revival starts in the hearts of His people, not in the headlines. But an untold number of believers do play an important role in the secular media. Let's support them in their efforts to be a light for Christ in their areas of influence. Then, when we do something that glorifies God, let's pray they will be in a position to influence positive coverage of whatever it is.

- *Failure to obey God's commands.* We cannot allow a victim's mentality to deter us from obedience. Christians must have the courage to do what is right whether we get a societal pat on the back or not. Consider Paul: The ever-present threat of being stoned or imprisoned would give anyone a victim's mentality. If I were Paul, I would have seriously considered reopening that tent-making shop and maybe teaching a Sunday-school class when I had time. But Paul never stopped being obedient to his calling, and he certainly never developed a victim's mentality.

- *Distraction from our spiritual goals.* When we start worrying exclusively about the ACLU instead of loving our neighbors and proclaiming the gospel, we have already lost the battle. Understand what I am saying before you get in a jumping-to-conclusions workout. I am not saying that we should ignore the ACLU or other significant groups and issues. I am suggesting that we have at times become so fixated on how others attempt to incapacitate our message that we are drawn into the fight and entirely away from the delivery of our message.

Victimization diminishes Christ. There is probably no way to say this without sounding smug and arrogant to people who do not believe in Jesus, but the truth is simply this: If what we believe is true (and I believe it is), then no amount of cultural contrariety will prevent God from accomplishing His plan. Christians who demonstrate the grace and sacrificial love of Christ can offset dozens of ACLU lawsuits banning Nativity scenes from the town square and Christmas carols from the public schools' "winter solstice" concerts. We must not allow cultural opposition to distract us and diminish our Lord.

2. Separatism

Separatism is an age-old struggle. How much *should* we remove ourselves from the "sinful world"? I would suggest the examples of Christ, Paul, and others in Scripture confirm that *balance* is the key word.

- *Separate doesn't mean isolate.* Christ said in Matthew 4:19, "Come, follow me...and I will make you fishers of men." I am not an expert fisherman, but I enjoy the activity. I have never (and you can quote me on this) caught a fish without going to the water where the fish were located. I have never had a single fish flop into my house on its own accord. Likewise, you cannot be fishers of men without going to where they are located. But understand this: Sometimes they will be in polluted water.

- *Separate from the things of the world, not the people of the world.* There are obviously a number of places that Christians should be wary of visiting and various activities that we should avoid. But that does not mean to avoid the people who frequent such places and participate in these activities. Paul addressed this issue in 1 Corinthians: "I have written you in my letter not to associate with sexually immoral people—not at all meaning the people of this world who are immoral, or the greedy and swindlers, or idolaters. In that case you would have to leave this world" (5:9-10). Paul understood that we would have to move to another planet if disassociating from sinners was the goal.

He was speaking of Christians who demonstrated these sinful traits, not the nonbelievers. He understood that in order to follow Jesus' command to "go into the world," we would have to initiate actual contact with the folks in that world.

3. Anti-Intellectualism

The anti-intellectual issue will be dealt with in some detail (and with itty-bitty words) in chapter 13.

A BETTER STRATEGY PART ONE: LOVE AND LISTEN

The believers of Acts did not feel the need to fight a culture war because they keenly expected to be with Jesus in heaven soon. When time is short, you cut to the chase. Rarely does anyone who knows he has a limited amount of time to live decide to crank up the office hours and work a little more. Most realize that family, friends, and faith are the important issues.

For the believers in the first century, the belief that time was short meant talking about the risen Savior. Caesar could go toss salads for all they cared because the only important issue was Jesus. It's safe to say that the early Christians enjoyed few social or political advantages, yet their zeal and genuine (key word: *genuine*) faith changed the world and the culture for millennia to come. More about that in chapter 15: Pleading Humanity.

No matter how strongly each of us feels about issues related to the worldview/culture war struggle, all of us Christians must exhibit grace. Too often we have come off as mean, condescending, and anti-intellectual. We must sear into our hearts and consciousness that the enemy is the conflicting worldview, not the people who hold that worldview. Certainly sincere Christians have heartfelt convictions and beliefs, but so do many outside of the faith. Sincerity and conviction are not exclusive franchises of Christianity. No matter how strongly you feel you are right, you cannot argue your way to success. Sadly, it always seems that the least informed make the most noise. Mark Twain made this wry observation: "Noise proves nothing. Often a hen who has merely laid an egg cackles as if she has laid an asteroid."

Too many of us are like the folks described in Acts 19:32: "The assembly was in confusion: Some were shouting one thing, some another." (A church board meeting?) But here comes the classic: "Most of the people did not even know why they were there."

Know why you are "there." Take the time to understand the issues. Take care of your responsibilities to Caesar but make sure you take care of your other citizenship requirements as well. Love the Lord your God with all your heart, mind, and body. Love your neighbor as yourself. Walk and talk the gospel and realize that "wisdom is proved right by her actions."

The book of James is one of my favorite in the Bible because of its profound common sense. James wrote, "Everyone should be quick to listen, slow to speak and slow to become angry, for man's anger does not bring about the righteous life that God desires" (1:19-20). Or as they say, God gave us two eyes, two ears, and one mouth. Which one might He have wanted us to use the least?

But when we're passionate about our beliefs, it's so easy to get riled up, jumping ahead of others in conversation instead of listening to them. We think we know where they are going with their "liberal" philosophies, so we interrupt to straighten them out. Try that communication strategy in your marriage. "I know what you are going to say, honey, so let's not bother with that and focus instead on why you are wrong." (Yeah, it doesn't work for me either.) Responding with grace in this graceless society will draw attention to Christ. It is not our job to defeat those we find ourselves in disagreement with. Instead, it is our job to speak the truth in love with respect, honor, and compassion for the listener—and then leave the results to God.

In Matthew 22, the apostle wrote about the reigning masters of the "let me tell you why you're wrong" school of debate when the Pharisees decided to challenge Jesus. I love what seems to be a mere aside in verse 34 when Matthew notes, "Hearing that Jesus had silenced the Sadducees, the Pharisees got together." Can't you just see it, the Pharisees strutting in like roosters to take over for the poor little overmatched Sadducees?

"Move over, boys! Time to let the real men take charge!"

The text tells us that an expert in the law (yep, a lawyer) tested Jesus with this question: "Which is the greatest commandment in the Law?" Christ, as always, confounded His accusers. The first commandment, He said, is to "love the Lord your God with all your heart and with all your soul and with all your mind. This is the first and greatest commandment" (verses 37-38). I'm sure the Pharisees puffed up on that one. But Jesus wasn't done. The airbags were about to be deflated. The second commandment, the Lord said, is to "love your neighbor as yourself. All the Law and the Prophets hang on these two commandments" (verses 39-40). That one was measurable. The Pharisees knew they fell short. You can't fake what you do with your time and resources and how you treat those around you. And the Pharisees couldn't gloss over the fact that Jesus used the word *commandment* for the love-your-neighbor thing. I imagine they went slinking away, accompanied by the snickering laugh track of the Sadducees, to plot another strategy for trapping Jesus.

I guarantee you that if I truly used those two simple commands as the yardstick for my life, I would be transformed, and God would use my life to transform those around me. Ask the average person who is the most important person in his life, and he is most likely to mention someone who has shown great love toward him. Mother Teresa was not revered for her wealth, intellect, or beauty, but for her incomprehensible love for the poor and downtrodden of Calcutta.

A BETTER STRATEGY PART TWO:
IT'S ALL IN THE DELIVERY

What if we decided to be a kinder and gentler Rambo, fearlessly and boldly confronting the culture with a great and incomprehensible love? I can tell you in advance that the results would be mixed. Acts 17 documents the apostle Paul's visit to the city of Athens, a city that caused him great distress (the Greek word, roughly translated, means "ticked off") because the city was full of idols. Yet, instead of arguing with or maligning the Jews and God-fearing Greeks, he *reasoned with* them and others who came to listen. Paul was introducing them to some strange ideas, and they wanted to know more. (Verse 21 notes that residents of Athens spent their time doing nothing but talking about and listening to the latest ideas. Their pastime could be considered an ancient version of our talk-radio format. Ditticus Rushii Limbaughius?) I love what happens next. Paul met his audience where they were. He stood up and said, "Men of Athens! I see that in every way you are very religious. For as I walked around and looked carefully at your objects of worship [notice no condemnation of the idols that Paul obviously found distasteful], I even found an altar with this inscription: TO AN UNKNOWN GOD. Now what you worship as something unknown I am going to proclaim to you" (verses 22-23).

Brilliant! In broadcasting this is known as packaging your idea. You set up a common interest and then tease the audience with the coming payoff to keep them tuned in. But what if Paul and the early believers had approached Athens with some of the strategies we use today? Several believers would march throughout the marketplace defiantly holding up placards:

IF YOU THINK YOU ARE STOIC NOW,
WAIT TILL THE LORD RETURNS!

HEY, EPICUREANS…THE PARTY'S OVER!

JUST WAIT TILL WE GET RID OF THESE SCROLLS
AND GET THE *KING JAMES VERSION…*
GOD'S OFFICIAL WORD! [I'm just kidding.]

What if Paul had stepped up and announced, "Repent, you pagan, godless sons of the devil, before you burn in a fiery hell. Take your idols and put them where the goddess of sunlight doesn't shine."

I don't think Paul would have had much of an audience, let alone success. When he finished speaking to the crowd in Athens, the Bible records the box score. It's pretty much what you and I can expect when we sincerely and lovingly explain our faith. Some of them sneered. (In response to this book, I expect to hear from this faction more than any other group.) Some of them said, "We want to hear you again on this subject." (My publisher wants to hear this one more often.) And a few "believed." (That is my prayer, along with hearing that a few recommitted to the faith.) Paul endured all that he did for those who believed and those who wanted to hear more. He could not have enjoyed the sneers. While that response is not unexpected, it is never fun.

The early church had no chance to "win" the culture war. Instead they built a community of believers that infiltrated the culture. Having an effect on the prevailing culture requires more than having the Ten Commandments in a courtroom. It requires more than reciting a prayer before a high-school football game. It requires more than having a Nativity scene in the city square. The Holy Spirit would not have left Ohio if the state were forced to remove "With God all things are possible" from the state seal. Affecting the culture means planting and nourishing a Christian worldview in the hearts and lives of your family, your neighbors, and your community.

So every believer is to build a foundation first on the solid rock of hearing Christ's words and then putting those teachings into practice, with no excuses. That does not mean doing so with no mistakes or failures. But when we fall short we take responsibility, repent, regroup, and reenter the fray. From that solid foundation I can build a marriage, a family, a church, a community, and a culture.

I have coached youth baseball for years. (If you still believe that human beings are inherently good, just go to kids' baseball or softball games. But I digress.) One of the things that drives me nuts is parents who shout the obvious and offer no suggestions. Little Freddy hits a foul ball. "Straighten it out, Freddy!" Dad yells. *No kidding,* Freddy thinks, *I thought I was supposed to hit it foul.* Then there's the parent who screams at Becky to "throw strikes," as if that has been ignored at practice sessions. *Really, Dad? Throw strikes? That hadn't crossed my mind.* What Freddie needs is help. Start the hands sooner. Open the hips. Pivot on the back foot. Try to hit the ball in front of the plate. "Straighten it out" doesn't help at all. Becky needs instruction. Stride further. Change your grip. Follow through.

But what these parents do is often what Christians do when confronting the moral issues of our culture. "STOP DOING THAT!" we scream. But the culture screams back at us, "HOW?" Or more likely, "WHY?" And answering those questions is our job. We must be able to tell them how. And we should be able to tell them why. Pick your battles prayerfully. Prepare yourself for the battle. Anything less than willingness to engage the world with truth and grace cheapens the veracity of our message.

BOOT CAMP 101:
HOW THE STRATEGIES PLAY OUT

What would it look like if we were to apply these strategies to our encounters with culture? Let's consider issues related to the sanctity of life, a cultural battlefront in which we must be engaged. It is easy for Christians to be intimidated by the venomous criticism pro-choice groups throw at us. The brilliant Christian philosopher (no, that's not an oxymoron) Francis Schaeffer identified abortion as the watershed issue of our era. Schaeffer wrote that, "Of all the subjects relating to the erosion of the sanctity of human life, abortion is the keystone. It is the first and crucial issue that has been overwhelming in changing attitudes toward the value of life in general." Back in the early '80s when he made that statement, I thought Schaeffer was overstating the issue a bit. Now I see that he was deadly accurate in every sense of the phrase.

Some quotes from current ethicists give me great cause for concern. Dr. Peter Singer is a lightning rod for conservatives and is widely quoted for his radical positions on infanticide. He believes, for example, that when a hemophiliac child is born the parents should have the right to decide whether to kill that child or to have another healthy child who is "likely to have a better life than the one killed." In his mind, the total amount of happiness for all involved will be greater if the disabled infant is killed. What a bizarre scale of justice Singer advocates, that we can somehow weigh happiness and sentence the loser to death. Singer states in his best-selling book *Practical Ethics,* "The loss of happy life for the first infant is outweighed by the gain of a happier life for the second." He goes on: "Therefore, if killing the hemophiliac infant has no adverse effect on others, it would, according to the total view, be right to kill him." He has been quoted as saying that "killing a disabled infant is not morally equivalent to killing a person."

In a book Singer coauthored with Helga Kuhse *(Should the Baby Live?),* they suggest that a period of twenty-eight days be allowed before a baby is accepted as having the same right to life as others. According to the authors, "This is clearly well before the infant could have a sense of its own existence over time, and would allow a couple to decide that it is better not to continue with a life that has begun very badly."

I shudder when I think that, in such an environment, Joni and I might have been pressured to terminate Katie's life within that twenty-eight-day window. Looking back, I think there is no way we would have done that. But in the heartbreak and distress of the moment, I am not totally sure. Certainly our moral standards would have told us it was wrong, and I can tell you the same thing unequivocally with the hindsight of actual experience. More on that to come.

I would like to dismiss Singer as an out-of-the-mainstream extremist in the ethical marketplace of ideas. But I cannot because of his influential position in our culture. Singer is the first full-time Professor of Bioethics at the University Center for Human Values at Princeton University. Princeton—the university that was founded by the great theologian and preacher Jonathon Edwards! Singer's *Practical Ethics* is an international bestseller and has been translated into fifteen languages. He is the most renowned proponent of utilitarianism, a philosophy that takes the position that the best moral action is the one that brings the greatest amount of pleasure and happiness to the greatest number of people. As Chuck Colson asks in his book *How Now Shall We Live?*, "What will happen when these elite students move into positions of power?" It is an important question. Singer has expanded his definition of nonpersons to include incompetent persons of all ages, whose families decide their lives are not worth living. And what a subjective decision that is. I can't forget that it was during my parents' lifetime that Germany, a country with a sizable Christian population, killed millions of "defectives" for the greater good. Can it happen here? God forbid. But we must never back off the belief that every life is intrinsically and divinely valuable. Call me crazy, but at least call me consistent.

Sanctity of life is one of several worldview issues over which Christians go head-to-head with the popular culture. Evolution versus Creation has become another cultural flash point, and it is an issue that has troubled me. Darwinists can make you feel very much like a transitional species if you believe in the Creator. After reading the works of writers like William Dembski *(Intelligent Design: The Bridge Between Science and Theology)* and Michael Behe *(Darwin's Black Box: The Biochemical Challenge to Evolution)*, I have a new confidence in the intellectual scholarship of the Creation position (and a headache). Phillip Johnson's *Darwin on Trial* is an excellent overview of the subject.

Truth as an absolute based on God's Word is another worldview foundational stone. As important as it is, Christians have too often compromised the integrity of biblical truth by dwelling on personal convictions (smoking, drinking, clothing, and so on) instead. Peter wrote that we should "Above all, love each other deeply, because love covers over a multitude of sins (1 Peter 4:8)." Our nature, however, is to have a multitude of issues that covers our love.

As believers we need to take the time to learn the basic worldviews and what they encompass. To understand how relativism creeps into the classroom, the workplace, and even the sanctuary. Chuck Colson and Nancy Pearcey outline these issues brilliantly in *How Now Shall We Live?* Understanding the Christian worldview is an important part of the armor if a believer's faith is to survive intact. For example, I try to balance *Time* with a newsmagazine like *World* that comes from a Christian worldview. I read *Christianity Today* along with *Newsweek*. I want to read all perspectives, but never at the expense of my Christian worldview.

The world is not our enemy. The world is where we live. The ungodly worldview of the culture is our foe. We need to be right in the middle of the world with something better to offer. Our culture is our common ground with everyone else, and we must be out there. Jesus went straight to those who needed His message most. Matthew wrote, "The Son of Man came eating and drinking, and they say, 'Here is a glutton and a drunkard, a friend of tax collectors and "sinners."'" (11:19). Of course the culture is immoral. Surprise! Even a cursory reading of Jesus' teachings would lead you to expect that. We need to begin to offer some well-reasoned answers instead of shocked indignation.

I want to wrap up this chapter with a recent item I read about the infamous Peter Singer. Recently he has been criticized for his alleged hypocrisy on the issues of euthanasia and what constitutes a person. He had drawn the line between persons (the ability to feel and reason, self-awareness, the ability to imagine a future) and nonpersons (comatose, severe Alzheimer's, and so on). Singer argues that life is not inherently valuable and that some lives are better off not being lived at all. He sees this as simply a "desire to avoid suffering." How very noble! But now comes the inconsistency of Dr. Singer's worldview. His mother is tragically stricken with Alzheimer's and by any standard she would fit into his definition of a nonperson. So how does Singer respond? Like a person who deep down in his soul believes in the dignity of life. He has spent significant amounts of money to care for his mother instead of sending that money to someone who could create more "overall" happiness as a "person."

Now, I don't want to come across as mean here. I support with all of my being Dr. Singer's obvious love for and his subsequent financial support of his mother. But this kind of behavior fits into my worldview, not his. Singer responded, "I think this has made me see how the issues of someone with these kinds of problems are really very difficult. Perhaps it is more difficult than I thought before, because it's different when it's your mother." When it became personal, Singer's worldview did not work. My critics will say that philosophy need not be autobiographical or even personal. But I can tell you that for this writer, philosophies that determine who is a "person" and who is not had better be valid for the philosopher as well as the philosophees!

Peter Singer's mother has value and should be cared for. Our daughter had value and deserved to be cared for. That is my worldview. I can live with mine.

Part III

Reality-Based Faith
for Survivors

Being Real in an Artificial World

Chapter 11

This Is a Hard Teaching!

If God is your Co-Pilot...switch seats.

—BUMPER STICKER

I have never liked movies about Jesus. I think the reason is that I can never get entirely comfortable with whomever the person is who plays Jesus. The actor never seems quite right. I don't want my Jesus to be effeminate, but then I don't want Him to be harsh or overly macho either. He must be good looking without being too pretty. I picture Him as tall, even though I know that is culturally unlikely. I usually don't like the actor's voice and delivery even though I really have no idea what Jesus sounded like. Frankly, if Jesus played Himself, I would probably be critical until I saw the credits.

Most of us have a mental image of Jesus based on the pictures we've seen in churches all our lives. He doesn't look much like a Middle Eastern Jew in those pictures or in my mind. No, I have Jesus looking more like a masculine, well-built Caucasian who inexplicably speaks English to His disciples. I have molded Jesus into my own American image of fair play and hard work instead of seeking to be molded into His revolutionary character.

I think that running Jesus through an American filter is one reason we have trouble understanding who He is. He doesn't fit our culture. Actually, He didn't fit into His culture all that comfortably either.

COME AGAIN?

In John 6:25-66, after miraculously feeding five thousand hungry people, Jesus taught the crowds at Capernaum. When the people asked what they must do to accomplish the work God requires, Jesus answered, "The work of God is this: to believe in the one he has sent" (verse 29). Instead of accepting Jesus' words, they asked Him, "What miraculous sign then will you give that we may see it and believe you? What will you do? Our forefathers ate the manna in the desert"—and griped about it, if you'll remember—"as it is written: 'He gave them bread from heaven to eat.'" These same folks had just witnessed a great miracle. Jesus fed multitudes with five small loaves of bread and two small fish. They might as well have said, "Great trick, Lord. When's the next show?"

Jesus reminds them that Moses gave them bread from heaven, but the Father gives true bread from heaven that gives life to the world. Jesus says that He is the bread of life and that "he who comes to me will never go hungry, and he who believes in me will never be thirsty. But as I told you, you have seen me and still you do not believe" (verses 35-36). Later, Jesus explains the Father's will, saying, "everyone who looks to the Son and believes in him shall have eternal life" (verse 40).

The Jews responded to Jesus according to human nature. They

began to grumble. They pointed out that this Jesus was merely the son of Joseph and Mary, whom they know from the local shuffle-board league (see the Really New Burchett Translation). Who did this whippersnapper think He was? Up until now this whole thing had been kind of cool—free food, a carnival atmosphere, and excitement that attracted big crowds to this new teacher. But Jesus began to thin the ranks.

> I am the living bread that came down from heaven.
> If anyone eats of this bread, he will live forever. This
> bread is my flesh, which I will give for the life of the
> world. (John 6:51)

Now things were getting weird, and the Jews began to argue among themselves: "How can this man give us his flesh to eat?" (verse 52). Of course Jesus was talking about the future. He would be giving His flesh over to a death on the cross and shedding His blood for the sins of the world. This is the basis of the Eucharist or Lord's Supper by which Christians remember Christ's sacrificial death. Jesus continued to contrast His listeners' forefathers, who ate manna and died, with those who would feed on the bread of life and live forever. I can imagine that their heads were now spinning: "On hearing it, many of his disciples said, 'This is a hard teaching. Who can accept it?'... Jesus said to them, 'Does this offend you?'" (verses 60-61). Later John reported that "from this time many of his disciples [in the generic sense, not the twelve] turned back and no longer followed him" (verse 66).

"This is a hard teaching." That is the part of Jesus' ministry that we have diminished. The words of Jesus are full of hard teachings.

Yet we have made Him almost benign, and Jesus was anything but that. I try to reconcile these hard teachings with my romantic version of the person Jesus was. When I first became a Christian, I pictured Jesus as kind of a humble and lovable teddy bear traveling around Galilee singing the lyrics of the song called "Peace Train" by the artist formerly known as Cat Stevens.

But Jesus was not a conductor on the peace train. If anything He was a renegade who pulled the emergency brake and upset the entire schedule. If you think Jesus is just a feel-good teacher who could be a self-help guru on *Oprah* today, try some of these teachings on for size:

> Blessed are the poor in spirit, for theirs is the kingdom of heaven. (Matthew 5:3)

Blessed are the poor in spirit? That just doesn't fit what I see on Christian television. And that doesn't fit the image we try to sell about Christianity.

> Blessed are you when people insult you, persecute you and falsely say all kinds of evil against you because of me. (Matthew 5:11)

I'll have to take this one on faith. It doesn't feel blessed.

> But I tell you, Do not resist an evil person. If someone strikes you on the right cheek, turn to him the other also. And if someone wants to sue you and take your tunic, let him have your cloak as well. If some-

one forces you to go one mile, go with him two
miles. Give to the one who asks you, and do not turn
away from the one who wants to borrow from you.

You have heard that it was said, "Love your
neighbor and hate your enemy." But I tell you: Love
your enemies and pray for those who persecute you,
that you may be sons of your Father in heaven. He
causes his sun to rise on the evil and the good, and
sends rain on the righteous and the unrighteous. If
you love those who love you, what reward will you
get? Are not even the tax collectors doing that? And
if you greet only your brothers, what are you doing
more than others? Do not even pagans do that?
(Matthew 5:39-47)

Okay, I've got some work to do here. I'll get back to you.

You hypocrites! Isaiah was right when he prophesied
about you: "These people honor me with their lips,
but their hearts are far from me." (Matthew 15:7-8)

I know Jesus was talking about the Pharisees, but I got nailed
by the ricochet.

"Are you still so dull?" Jesus asked them. "Don't you
see that whatever enters the mouth goes into the
stomach and then out of the body? But the things
that come out of the mouth come from the heart, and
these make a man 'unclean.' For out of the heart come

> evil thoughts, murder, adultery, sexual immorality,
> theft, false testimony, slander. These are what make a
> man 'unclean'; but eating with unwashed hands does
> not make him 'unclean.'" (Matthew 15:16-20)

But Lord…it's so much easier to be legalistic than to change my heart and actions.

> Then Jesus said to his disciples, "If anyone would
> come after me, he must deny himself and take up
> his cross and follow me." (Matthew 16:24)

I must be honest. I haven't always been willing to deny myself. Correction: I am seldom willing to deny myself. Self-denial is not an attractive concept until you reach a point where you realize that the self you have been following is just not worth it. And I think when you talk candidly to a large number of my generation (Boomers), you realize that many of us are at or approaching that point.

> Then Peter came to Jesus and asked, "Lord, how
> many times shall I forgive my brother when he sins
> against me? Up to seven times?"
> Jesus answered, "I tell you, not seven times, but
> seventy-seven times." (Matthew 18:21-22)

I relate to Peter. He was feeling all good about himself. Feelin' spiritual. "I'll impress the Lord because seven times is pretty impressive." As usual, Jesus pierced to the core issue. Forgiveness is not about numbers; it's about the willingness to forgive.

> I tell you that anyone who divorces his wife, except
> for marital unfaithfulness, and marries another
> woman commits adultery. (Matthew 19:9)

Hey, folks, I didn't say it. The sad truth is that Christians are tolerant. Unfortunately we have become tolerant of the wrong things. I'm not judging my divorced brothers and sisters, but we have to admit that the church has become amazingly more tolerant about divorce in the past twenty years. We seem to cherry pick the sins that we tolerate less. Situational sanctimony does not honor Christ either.

> Woe to you, teachers of the law and Pharisees, you
> hypocrites! You clean the outside of the cup and
> dish, but inside they are full of greed and self-
> indulgence. Blind Pharisee! First clean the inside
> of the cup and dish, and then the outside also will
> be clean. (Matthew 23:25-26)

We clean up the outside of our lives (for the sake of those whose opinions don't really matter) and leave the inside dirty (for the One who matters most). We are often just as blind as the Pharisees. In other words, too blind to see it.

> Still another said, "I will follow you, Lord; but first
> let me go back and say good-by to my family."
> Jesus replied, "No one who puts his hand to the
> plow and looks back is fit for service in the king-
> dom of God." (Luke 9:61-62)

This is a hard teaching! We simply do not emphasize the cost of following Jesus. Yes, grace is free. But we sometimes make it cheap as well.

> Then Jesus said to his host, "When you give a luncheon or dinner, do not invite your friends, your brothers or relatives, or your rich neighbors; if you do, they may invite you back and so you will be repaid. But when you give a banquet, invite the poor, the crippled, the lame, the blind, and you will be blessed. Although they cannot repay you, you will be repaid at the resurrection of the righteous." (Luke 14:12-14)

Can we move on? Jesus expects more from us if we decide to be listed among His followers. These are hard teachings. Who can accept them? And when Jesus asks, "Does this offend you?," what is the answer?

JESUS VERSUS THE AMERICAN DREAM

One of the areas that the church awkwardly stumbles on today is how to deal with the incredible wealth possessed by our country. Jesus made it pretty clear what the priorities were to be.

> Now a man came up to Jesus and asked, "Teacher, what good thing must I do to get eternal life?"
> "Why do you ask me about what is good?" Jesus replied. "There is only One who is good. If you want to enter life, obey the commandments."

"Which ones?" the man inquired.

Jesus replied, "'Do not murder, do not commit adultery, do not steal, do not give false testimony, honor your father and mother,' and 'love your neighbor as yourself.'"

"All these I have kept," the young man said. "What do I still lack?" (Matthew 19:16-20)

I always found his second question interesting. In his mind he measured up to all the things the Lord listed. He didn't commit adultery, steal, or give false testimony. He honored his father and mother and he loved his neighbors as himself. It sounds like he lived a pretty good life, the kind of life many of us feel should get us safely inside the gate. Yet the young man knew something was missing. Something else was wrong. Jesus already knew what he was unwilling to give up.

Jesus answered, "If you want to be perfect, go, sell your possessions and give to the poor, and you will have treasure in heaven. Then come, follow me." (Matthew 19:21)

I've often wondered whether the Lord was just looking for the man's willingness to part with his riches. But it was obvious that this wasn't an option for this man. In his mind he had too much to lose.

When the young man heard this, he went away sad, because he had great wealth. (Matthew 19:22)

I am sympathetic to the young man. In fact, in many ways I *am* the young man (with gray hair). By the standards of the world I have great wealth. And I have not been willing enough to give that up for the Lord.

> Jesus looked around and said to his disciples, "How
> hard it is for the rich to enter the kingdom of God!"
> (Mark 10:23)

That's a little troubling to me. Why is it hard? Is it because rich people have harder hearts? Is it because the rich are not good people? Not at all. It is simply human nature for us to focus on wealth and possessions, leaving little room for dependence on God. Jesus understood that. When the money is rolling in from my television sports-directing career, I admit my trust in God to provide is a token courtesy. But when a strike that might eliminate a baseball season looms, my dependence upon Him and my earnestness in prayer increase dramatically. We are blessed beyond comparison in this country, but that same prosperity is also a curse. Wealth has created a culture of self-idolization that diminishes our daily need to trust God. When all our needs are self-provided (in our minds), God becomes the supplementary insurance package to our primary self-coverage.

> Someone in the crowd said to him, "Teacher,
> tell my brother to divide the inheritance
> with me."
> Jesus replied, "Man, who appointed me a judge
> or an arbiter between you?" (Luke 12:13-14)

This one makes me chuckle. Even Jesus doesn't want to get in the middle of a family fightin' over money!

> Then he said to them, "Watch out! Be on your guard
> against all kinds of greed; a man's life does not consist
> in the abundance of his possessions." (Luke 12:15)

I can guarantee that if an angel came to me at this moment and gave me the choice of godly children and grandchildren or great success and wealth, I would take the godly family in a heartbeat. And that is what Jesus is trying to teach us concerning money and possessions.

> And do not set your heart on what you will eat or
> drink; do not worry about it. For the pagan world
> runs after all such things, and your Father knows
> that you need them. But seek his kingdom, and
> these things will be given to you as well.
> Do not be afraid, little flock, for your Father has
> been pleased to give you the kingdom. Sell your pos-
> sessions and give to the poor. Provide purses for your-
> selves that will not wear out, a treasure in heaven that
> will not be exhausted, where no thief comes near and
> no moth destroys. For where your treasure is, there
> your heart will be also. (Luke 12:29-34)

Where is our treasure? That is the question all of us must address. For it is surely true that our heart will be there also. The *Los Angeles Times* recently reported that although churches are collecting more, church members are contributing smaller percentages of their income. Studies show that in 1998 churchgoers gave only 2.52 percent of after-tax income. This giving percentage was lower than it was in 1933 during the depths of the Depression. That, my Christian friends, is pathetic!

And it gives us an unfortunate clue as to where our treasure might be. These numbers were from a report written by Sylvia and John L. Ronsvalle (*The State of Church Giving Through 1998*, Empty Tomb, Inc.). The Ronsvalles' report states that "leadership in the church is committed to institutional maintenance and is abandoning church members to an agenda of a consumer lifestyle." What that means is the preponderance of church budgets are going to salaries and buildings while church members pile up credit debt and material possessions. Because the money left over for outreach is shrinking, the church is becoming more and more impotent outside of the church structures.

The report suggests that if current trends continue, the church will be "spending little to nothing on others by the middle of this century." God forbid that we allow that to happen. If churchgoers had given an average of 10 percent in 1998, another $131 billion would have been available for the Lord's work. You don't have to look far to see how much that could help in a world where people are dying for lack of life's necessities. Even worse, they die without experiencing the message of God's love, which Christians could likely provide with even modest sacrifice. But we must be willing to relinquish at least a little bit of our American dream, which has somehow morphed into an American right to possessions.

In Matthew, Jesus talks about reaching out to the least of our brothers as a sign of service to Him.

"For I was hungry and you gave me something to eat,
I was thirsty and you gave me something to drink, I
was a stranger and you invited me in, I needed clothes
and you clothed me, I was sick and you looked after
me, I was in prison and you came to visit me."

Then the righteous will answer him, "Lord,
when did we see you hungry and feed you, or
thirsty and give you something to drink? When did
we see you a stranger and invite you in, or needing
clothes and clothe you? When did we see you sick
or in prison and go to visit you?"

The King will reply, "I tell you the truth, whatever you did for one of the least of these brothers of
mine, you did for me." (Matthew 25:35-40)

Notice that the passage *does not say*, "For I was hungry and you
gave a check to the local food bank, I was thirsty and you gave
money to a relief fund, I was a stranger and you supported a
homeless shelter, I needed clothes and you made a quick drop-off
at Goodwill, I was sick and you donated to a Christian medical
outreach, I was in prison and you supported Prison Fellowship."
There is nothing wrong with doing any or all of the above, but I
would suggest we all need to mix in a little personal contact.

I have made a personal commitment in this area: I am committed to giving something besides money to the cause of Christ.
There is a time to give money to charity and a time to give of yourself. You won't get the same kind of blessings or personal growth
out of sending a check from the safety of the office that you would
rolling up your sleeves and actually touching someone. Yeah, I'm

too busy too. Yeah, it makes me uncomfortable. Yeah, I would rather be safely at home. Early in this book I talked about getting out of our comfort bunkers. This is an area I'll have to deal with myself in the coming months and years. But the truth is that every time I get off my rumpus and go serve others, I feel great. Yet time after time I forget that and retreat back to the bunker.

I saw an advertisement for World Vision that stated they could feed and clothe a child for $26 a month. At the time I was spending that much or more per month on grande venti mondo fifty-five gallon drum barrels of gourmet coffee drinks at the local legal stimulant store. I decided to curb my expensive caffeine fix and use that money to support a child. I am now helping a beautiful little seven-year-old in Guatemala. Frankly, I didn't give up a whole heck of a lot. I just allow a little extra time to brew my coffee at home before I hit the road. But it's a start. And the good feeling gets contagious and begins to spread to the rest of your spending if you stay faithful.

GOOD OLD-FASHIONED HARD WORK

Many people who call themselves Christians are good people who are leading good lives and sincerely trying to do good things. They go to Sunday school most of the time, coach youth soccer, give to the United Way, pay taxes, and so on and so on. Ask these folks if they believe they are going to heaven. Many who say yes reason that they will be judged on the preponderance of evidence. If the good outweighs the bad, they're in.

That makes sense to our American mind-set. It seems fair. In a society where we like to believe that if you work hard and keep trying you will succeed, then getting to heaven with the same program seems about right. There is only one problem. That is not what Jesus said. When asked in Luke if only a few would be saved, Jesus replied with an illustration.

> "Many, I tell you, will try to enter and will not be able to. Once the owner of the house gets up and closes the door, you will stand outside knocking and pleading, 'Sir, open the door for us.'
>
> "But he will answer, 'I don't know you or where you come from.'
>
> "Then you will say, 'We ate and drank with you, and you taught in our streets.'
>
> "But he will reply, 'I don't know you or where you come from. Away from me, all you evildoers!'"
> (Luke 13:24-27)

This is a hard teaching! And when Jesus asks, "Does this offend you?," the answer from many would be yes. This is not what we want to hear. But it begs a fundamental question: Is Jesus Christ who He said He was? If yes, then we must address the ramifications. For believers, it will mean making the commitment to implement all of Christ's teachings in our lives. Even the hard ones.

> But I tell you that men will have to give account on the day of judgment for every careless word they have spoken. For by your words you will be acquitted, and by your words you will be condemned.
> (Matthew 12:36-37)

This statement makes me extremely tense. As you might have surmised from reading this book, I have produced a litany of careless words over my lifetime. If I have to give an account for every one of them, you might want to stay out of my line. It will not be the express lane! I have this nightmare that God has a VCR cued up with all those remarks that I thought were funny. He replays what I said and then I hear this booming, "Thought that was pretty funny, huh?" I know that's not going to happen. I know my careless words are covered by Christ's redemptive act. Still, pondering the possibility of a heavenly replay of my words tends to make me at least a bit more thoughtful.

The topic of "bad" words is an interesting one for Christians. We abhor bad language on television and movies. I personally find the gratuitous use of certain words offensive. I particularly find the use of God's name in oaths offensive. Again though, while I have the right to kindly object on the grounds of civility, I have no expectations that my worldview as a Christian will be honored by non-Christians. I still think we have to earn that respect through a life that reflects Christ. We fight the wrong battles and lose the war.

Simply understanding that others don't always comprehend your worldview can open doors as well. In my profession as a sports director I encounter a large volume of crude humor and coarse language. I have learned not to expect high standards from those I work around. I worked with a network producer who began making jokes about "God Squadders."

"Easy," I said jokingly.

"Why?" he asked. "Are you a God Squadder too?"

"Yes, I am."

"You mean you're a born again?" (He had learned some of our language.)

"Yes."

"Well, I hope my language hasn't offended you," he said.

"Your language has nothing to do with my faith in Christ," I told him. "Your language is an issue of civility and good manners. It doesn't offend me because of my faith."

He looked a little stunned.

"I'd like to discuss that with you some time," he finally said.

"I would love to."

I guarantee you he would not have been interested in my faith if I had been judgmental or condemning about his language because of my Christianity. I am responsible for me. I cannot expect others to honor my convictions if they don't have my relationship and faith in God.

We believers often engage in our own brand of Christian cussing. How many times have you heard a religious person toss out a "darn it" with the same intensity and spirit of the earthier version? What's the difference? Over the years I have heard wonderful creativity in Christian cussing. "Dadgum" and "Jiminy Cricket" are among the best. My personal favorite is "Godfrey Daniels!" While I find that better than using the Lord's name in vain, I contend it's the attitude that counts spiritually. The actual words are merely cultural civility. But let's be honest: If your heart harbors the same anger, you might as well get your money's worth.

I've often wondered where using the name of Jesus Christ came into play when you hit your thumb with a hammer. Imagine screaming some other religious leader's name when you bump your head.

"Dalai Lama!"

Silly, huh?

Perhaps part of your quest for good manners and civility would be dropping all expletives from your vocabulary. It will only make you look more intelligent. Try and reserve the name of Jesus for seeking truth and teachings. God does not have a last name. You can thank me in eternity.

> Make a tree good and its fruit will be good, or
> make a tree bad and its fruit will be bad, for a tree
> is recognized by its fruit. You brood of vipers,
> how can you who are evil say anything good?
> For out of the overflow of the heart the mouth
> speaks. The good man brings good things out of
> the good stored up in him, and the evil man
> brings evil things out of the evil stored up in
> him. (Matthew 12:33-35)

This is another hard teaching. It is time for believers to stop characterizing Jesus like the SNL character Stuart Smalley and his *Daily Affirmation.* You've heard the bit: "You're good enough, you're smart enough, and doggone it, people like you!" When you accept Christ's redemption, you are good enough. You have unique spiritual gifts from God. People may or may not always like you if you speak the truth, even in love. But doggone it, you must begin to implement all of His teachings, not just the easy ones. Nothing truly worthwhile is easy. Excellence in any endeavor takes hard work and discipline. Can the things of eternal excellence require any less?

Chapter 12

Six Things I Learned About Evangelism During Election 2000

*Under certain circumstances, profanity provides a relief
denied even to prayer.*

—MARK TWAIN

I'm no advocate of profanity, but the United States 2000 presidential election gave a certain appeal to Twain's sentiments. The Comedy Central Network called the millennium election "Indecision 2000" months before the advent of the November nonsense. (Were they ever prophetic!) Sometime during day thirty-seven of glassy-eyed cable-news name-calling, I experienced an epiphany. Suddenly I realized that everything I ever needed to know about evangelism I could learn from this aberration, this election that should have used the *Benny Hill* theme as its soundtrack. If ever there was a compelling argument about why Christians should put their trust in God and not government, it was this traveling circus.

167

As the election process crept forward at an agonizing pace, I sat slack-jawed at what I heard on the cable news networks. (I have long since given up on the major networks as a source of actual facts.) After just a few weeks of vote counting, I had learned the bent of most of the Sound Bite Players (politicians and pundits), and I could predict each interviewee's strategy, tone, and responses before the interview began. Certain people earned my less-than-coveted Mute Award. As everyone babbled on, I realized that Christians face many of the same communication quandaries when we try to talk to others about our beliefs. And I realize that I am at risk of offending even more people now by diving into the volatile mix of politics and religion. (Perhaps I can throw in sex somewhere and watch this whole chapter spontaneously combust.) Nevertheless, here are the six things that I learned from my cable television course on the electoral college.

LESSON ONE:
PEOPLE HEAR WHAT THEY WANT TO HEAR AND SEE WHAT THEY WANT TO SEE

It amazes me that two intelligent and decent people can look at the same incident or set of facts and end up vehemently 180 degrees opposite in how they see it. For example, five days before Election Day, the revelation of a DUI charge from twenty-four years ago sent Texas Governor George W. Bush's chances for victory into a tailspin. Governor Bush had not revealed the details of the arrest to the media and the public. According to some breathless reports, he had only "vaguely" referenced or "merely hinted" at the offense and had not been forthcoming with the "truth."

Seen and Heard by Me

I am a supporter of George W. Bush, so when he said earlier in the campaign that he had a problem with drinking and had to quit cold turkey, I understood what that meant. When Mr. Bush was quoted as saying, "The bottle had become bigger than me," I *heard* that as a brave and bold admission. I *saw* a man who was willing to admit weakness, courageous enough to confess it, and strong enough to confront it. I did not need to know the details of every time he threw up or was bombastic at a party. I have been around drinkers enough to have a general idea. (I might have even been "overserved" a time or two, but that would have been before 1974, and I really *didn't* inhale.)

Seen and Heard by Others

Those who opposed Mr. Bush *heard* "cover-up." They *saw* a man who said one thing about integrity and did another. One Web site had several pages of comments all under the heading of "hypocrite." *Slate E-Zine's* Jacob Weisberg described Dubya's "off-the-charts hypocrisy" in a scathing indictment of the incident. I had friends outside of Texas who seemed to believe that Austin was a hazard because the governor was careening crazily down city streets in his pickup truck tossing Lone Star Longnecks out the cab rear window.

Actor Martin Sheen proclaimed that he thought Governor Bush was a "white-knuckle drunk" who was "still in denial about it." According to Mr. Sheen you have got to be "in a program." He added that he did not mean to insult Governor Bush, and I'm sure no apologies were needed. After all, who amongst us minds being publicly called a "white-knuckle drunk" fourteen years after you quit drinking by someone who doesn't even know you? Writer

Joan Didion mocked the governor in a feature article for *The New York Review of Books.* She reported his quote that "the main reason I quit was because I accepted Jesus Christ as my personal savior in 1986." Didion responded, "Amazing isn't it, that there are people who really talk like that?"

Application

Jesus said in Matthew 13:13, "This is why I speak to them in parables: 'Though seeing, they do not see; though hearing, they do not hear or understand.'" We who have faith in God also hear what we want to hear. We choose to ignore the issues that might create discomfort or doubt when we should be confronting them with a confidence born of faith.

We do not fulfill our commission to spread the gospel when we refuse to hear the doubters, the skeptics, and their criticisms. We blame the devil, the culture, and the media for everything when perhaps we should prayerfully listen to what is being said and discerningly sort through it for some better ways to represent our Lord and reach out to others.

Those who are opposed to God see only the hypocrites and the ridiculous fringe players. The unbelievers' cacophony of criticism blocks their ability to hear the caring voices of millions of sincere Christians who serve selflessly and lovingly around the world.

When you express your beliefs to others, expect them to hear what they want to hear. It is not the norm to meet someone who is spiritually ready to listen to and comprehend everything you have to say. Most of the time you are merely planting seeds to be nurtured by others. Or perhaps you can tear down a brick or two from their wall of objections. Be patient. Understand that they may not necessarily hear all of what you are saying, but they may be hearing part of it. Love them, be kind, and live a life that will generate interest and give you a platform to talk further.

LESSON TWO: TONE DICTATES RECEPTION

Mere weeks after Election Day, civil discourse seemed an impossible dream. Fifty percent of the population was screaming that Governor Bush stole the election. Fifty percent of the country was screaming that Vice President Gore was trying to steal it. In the midst of all the screaming, what folks were actually trying to say was grossly obscured. Consider the brouhaha surrounding a column written by Democratic commentator Paul Begala.

What He Said He Meant

Because I had the advantage of reading Begala's defense of the column before I read the original piece, I will start there. Begala claimed he was mugged by the zealots, though I guess you rarely get mugged by the apathetic. His subtitle noted how critics got his comments completely and alarmingly wrong. Begala stated that he was simply trying to show the complexities of our society and that any fair-minded person would see that.

What I Read

Reading his defense first left me a little wiggle room as I prepared to read his column. Either I would agree with him and emerge "fair-minded," or I would turn out to be a narrow-minded, slope-foreheaded cretin (or, by his standards, a Republican). I tried to not let his description of columnist Peggy Noonan as a pretentious and tendentious writer affect my judgment. I tried to not let the fact that I had to look up *tendentious* in the dictionary puncture my pride. (For my fellow morons *tendentious* means "a partisan, implicit and even controversial point of view.") I tried to overlook Begala's description of writer and pundit Robert Novak as the prince of darkness himself. And I tried to carefully review the intent of his column in light of his clarification.

The title of Begala's piece was "Banana Republicans." It was a response to a column by commentator Mike Barnicle that explored how United States politics is geographically divided. Barnicle was commenting on the famous map that showed seas of red (Republican) across the Heartland, South, and Rockies, while strips of blue (Democrat) lay along the coasts and in large union cities and states.

Begala opened with, "The Bushies are desperate." And then, "They're saying some really stupid things." Now, when you have been called desperate and stupid in the first two sentences, it takes a great deal of grace to mine for pearls of wisdom. But let's read on. Begala noted that "[Republicans] seem to care more about their preferred outcome than an honest and fair process." He also said Republicans "crave power more than they respect democracy." He added dishonesty, greed, power hunger, and lack of patriotism to the list of Republicans' charming attributes. I understand that commentators are paid to elicit an emotional response. But the tone Mr. Begala took hardly set the stage for any potential meeting of the minds.

Barnicle had pointed out the amount of territory that Governor Bush had carried in the election (denoted by red) versus the states supporting Mr. Gore (shaded in blue). Barnicle cited this as proof of America's cultural "Wal-Mart versus Martha Stewart" divide. Begala disagreed, and in his attempts to demonstrate that Middle America "is a much more complicated place than the Northeastern elite wants to admit," he wrote, "Barnicle is right when he notes that tens of millions of good people in Middle America voted Republican. But if you look closely at that map you see a more complex picture. You see the state where James Byrd was lynch-dragged behind a pickup truck until his body came apart—it's red. You see the state where Matthew Shepard was crucified on a split-rail fence for the crime of being gay—it's red. You see the state where right-wing extremists blew up a federal office building and murdered scores of federal employees—it's red. The state where an Army private who was thought to be gay was bludgeoned to death with a baseball bat, and the state where neo-Nazi skinheads murdered two African-Americans because of their skin color, and the state where Bob Jones University spews its anti-Catholic bigotry: they're all red too."

Golly, Paul, how could we thin-skinned conservatives take offense at that?

Begala's concluding point is that "Middle America is a far more complicated place than even a gifted commentator like Mike Barnicle gives us credit for. It's not all just red and blue—or black and white." His last point is in fact well taken. Values are not confined to particular states or regions represented by colors. Hate is liable to turn up anywhere. Good and bad people live in all sections of our land.

Application

My point in all of this is to show how the tone of discourse influences what is heard or read by your audience. If Mr. Begala was sincerely trying to make a serious point (and I have no particular reason to doubt him), it was lost to at least 50 percent of his audience by the tone of his initial comments and the over-the-top excess of his examples.

For Christians the lesson is simple. Our tone affects our communication. Screaming at people and calling them sinners and degenerates may work on rare occasions. I once caught a salmon in Puget Sound by wrapping the fishing line around his tail, so in effect, I lassoed a fish (witnesses available upon request). It brought in the catch, but I will surely never do it again. Most people react to angry and condemnatory Christians much like political conservatives responded to Paul Begala's column. Begala's final and most important point was unheard.

I believe in the doctrine of sin. I believe we must be candid about people's separation from God. I believe the answer to that separation is faith in Jesus Christ. But the tone and attitude of our discourse is important. Notice that Christ saved His anger and venom for the hypocritical religious types, not those seeking faith or even those who didn't profess faith at all. "Woe to you, teachers of the law and Pharisees, you hypocrites!" Jesus said in one of His many in-your-face encounters with the religious leaders. "You shut the kingdom of heaven in men's faces. You yourselves do not enter, nor will you let those enter who are trying to" (Matthew 23:13-14).

Jesus was just warming up.

> "Woe to you, teachers of the law and Pharisees, you
> hypocrites! You travel over land and sea to win a
> single convert, and when he becomes one, you
> make him twice as much a son of hell as you are."
> (Matthew 23:15)

Jesus clearly did get personal with the religious types.

> "You snakes! You brood of vipers! How will you
> escape being condemned to hell?" (Matthew 23:33)

That quote coming from Jesus would have made me more than a little tense. There are more examples, but I think you get the point. Jesus reserved a different tone for the religious types who weren't living the life. Contrast that to how He communicated to those without faith. One of the Bible's most amazing demonstrations of grace is when the woman who was caught in sin was brought before Jesus. Jesus showed love, compassion, and grace where none had been shown to her before. You know the story. No one had the guts to cast the first stone. Sadly, I'm afraid that today a lot of Christians would be in the windup before Jesus finished the question. But none did on that day.

> Jesus straightened up and asked her, "Woman,
> where are they? Has no one condemned you?"
>   "No one, sir," she said.
>   "Then neither do I condemn you," Jesus declared.
> "Go now and leave your life of sin." (John 8:10-11)

Compare the stinging rebukes directed toward the religious hypocrites with Christ's tender acceptance of a criminal executed by his side.

> One of the criminals who hung there hurled insults
> at him: "Aren't you the Christ? Save yourself and us!"

But the other criminal rebuked him. "Don't you fear God," he said, "since you are under the same sentence? We are punished justly, for we are getting what our deeds deserve. But this man has done nothing wrong."

Then he said, "Jesus, remember me when you come into your kingdom."

Jesus answered him, "I tell you the truth, today you will be with me in paradise." (Luke 23:39-43)

Jesus was always kind in tone and tender in His acceptance of seeking sinners.

Tone dictates reception. A loving and caring tone may not always bring results, but I can assure you it will increase the chances of being heard.

LESSON THREE:
PARTISAN PEOPLE GET PERSONAL

By November 8, it became apparent that the presidential decision would hinge on the disputed Florida outcome. The attorneys soon outnumbered alligators in the Sunshine State, and allegations flew thick as the legendary Florida Lovebugs that cloud the skies every spring and fall. Democratic demands for a hand recount of the ballots were heard everywhere.

What I Saw
Florida's Republican Secretary of State Katherine Harris halted the hand counts because the law specifically called for hand recounts only

for machine malfunctions or voter fraud, and neither of those reasons was claimed. She determined that the mandatory machine recount (as required by law) plus the absentee ballots would be certified as official results. While I certainly saw issues that needed to be addressed for future elections, the decision offered by the secretary of state seemed to be the best resolution for a far less-than-perfect situation. What happened next is an example of the "scorched earth" approach to dealing with frustrations that is becoming distressingly more common in our society. When we get angry we attack the person along with, or often instead of, the facts in question.

What Happened

Almost immediately Gore spokesman Chris Lehane called Mrs. Harris a "crony of Jeb Bush" and a "lackey for the Bush campaign." She was also called a "Stalinist" and a "Soviet Commissar." That was sadly predictable; such attacks are part of the new rules of politics. The troubling direction that philosophical dissent is taking was represented by two of our nation's most reputable newspapers. Did they stick to debate concerning the point of law regarding Mrs. Harris's decision or even what her motivation might be? Hardly. If civility was on life support, it officially died in November 2000 with comments like these. I have added my comments to the text.

The *Boston Globe* described her as "Florida's ghoulishly made-up secretary of state.... Her mask of mascara and eye shadow cannot hide the obvious. *[Excuse me? The obvious? What could she be trying to hide with the mascara? Let's read on.]* Ambition empowers her to hide behind the letter of the law."

Okay, I have issues here. First, her makeup has nothing to do with the evaluation of her actions, and a newspaper of this stature should know better. Second, since when is going by the letter of the law a *weakness* for a secretary of state?

Another great paper, the *Washington Post,* sank to similar lows: "Her lips were overdrawn with berry-red lipstick—the creamy sort that smears all over a coffee cup and leaves smudges on a shirt collar. *[Clear off the shelf space for the Pulitzer. This is some great reporting.]* Her skin had been plastered and powdered to the texture of pre-war walls in need of a skim coat *[?????]*. And her eyes, rimmed in liner and frosted with blue shadow, bore the telltale homogeneous spikes *[when I see those homogeneous spikes I know for sure]* of false eyelashes. Caterpillars seemed to rise and fall with every bat of her eyelid *[?????]*, with every downward glance to double-check— before reading—her latest 'determination.' *[Hang on! Like a good trial lawyer, the writer is about to bring into evidence the relevance of this line of reasoning]*. One wonders how this Republican woman, who can't even use restraint when she's wielding a mascara wand, will manage to…make sound decisions."

Aha! The well-documented mascara-wand link to solid reasoning. All women should be mascara-wand tested before being awarded an important position in society. Please! If that is the case, then men with ridiculous comb-overs should be similarly described: "One wonders how this Republicrat man, who can't even use restraint when he's wielding a hairbrush, will manage to…make sound decisions."

USA Today declared that Harris "might be more comfortable passing finger sandwiches at an art gala than managing affairs of state." How could the women of America allow such Neanderthal comments to go unchallenged? The ever-edifying Paul Begala weighed in early on Secretary Harris by saying "she looked like

Cruella de Vil coming to steal the puppies." However, I'm sure we misunderstood what he was really trying to say. Probably something about how complex our voting process really is.

Application

As I watched the ugly campaign of 2000 unfold, I realized that we tend to get personal when our ox is gored or we get bushwhacked (sorry). It was clear that angry and frustrated Gore supporters said ugly and unnecessary things. Bush supporters did exactly the same.

Once again, we believers in Christ do the same thing. When someone says something derogatory about our beliefs or faith, we are prone to show our insecurity by lashing out. We can be condescending: "Someday you will come to Jesus." Sometimes we are ugly: "Lord, open the eyes of this sinner." We can be accusatory and smug: "You took God out of the schools, and you are getting what you deserve." We can even be threatening: "Someday you will wish you had listened, my friend." We can be heartless: "AIDS is your punishment from God." We can be gleeful in our use of hell as the ultimate fate for those who oppose us. We need to be praying for everyone to be drawn to Christ, not relishing in their damnation. That is a human and sinful revenge response born out of pride.

"Make fun of me, huh? Then you will burn in hell." Yes, I have heard comments like that over the years. I must confess I have had similar thoughts. Hopefully I have experienced personal growth in that area. It doesn't bother me much anymore if someone makes fun of me and my beliefs. (I don't encourage it, but I will still endeavor to value you as a creation of God.) It is hard to pray for those who oppose you or would do harm to you. But that is what we are asked to do by our Lord in Matthew.

> Give to the one who asks you, and do not turn
> away from the one who wants to borrow from you.
> You have heard that it was said, "Love your neigh-
> bor and hate your enemy." But I tell you: Love your
> enemies and pray for those who persecute you.
> (Matthew 5:42-44)

Anyone can love Mr. Rogers. It is a little harder to care about Larry Flynt. But we Christians don't have the option of picking the people we want to love.

So don't get personal when people attack the faith. And don't get defensive when people attack our Lord. Why do we fall for that bait? A far better way to defend the truth of God's love is to demonstrate His love to those who show no grace in return. That is different. That stands out. We need to model what a relationship with God looks like in this messed up world. God (I am very sure) can handle Himself without our overreactions and defensive posturing. We need to show something different from the rest of the world by responding with assured dignity.

LESSON FOUR:
DIVERSION DOESN'T WORK FOR DOUBT

Our oldest son is a master of diversion. When he senses that his argument is slipping, he immediately diverts to some ancillary and often bizarre argument designed to confuse the issue until he regroups. He understands the power of momentum, and diverting derails momentum. You know this—I covered the basic idea in chapter 3. During my Election 101 course, I saw this technique used to perfection by the Gore team as they desperately tried to regroup.

What They Said

Within hours of the closing of the polls in Florida, we heard a dizzying array of charges. The butterfly ballot had confused thousands of voters and was blatantly unfair. Campaign official Donna Brazile announced that black voters had been harassed and kept away from the polls by police roadblocks and even police dogs. Gore's people stated over and over that the vice president had won the national popular vote. Therefore it was even more critical to restore all the "disenfranchised" votes (definition: those for Gore) to find the "will of the people." A full-page ad purchased by the vp's supporters in the *New York Times* declared that the voting results had been "nullified" and made the puzzling claim that the Florida recount fiasco threatened "our entire political process." Jesse Jackson was buzzing over Florida collecting evidence (that three months later no one had seen) about "intimidation" at the polls. Within just a day or two, it seemed that Florida was one big Hazard County and Boss Hogg was the election chief.

What I Saw

The Democrats had some compelling concerns, and I understood their frustration. But their legitimate concerns got lost in the flurry of accusations. Or was the whirlwind of charges simply designed to keep Katherine Harris from waving her evil mascara wand and sprinkling certification dust over the results? What I saw was that the infamous Palm Beach ballot was designed by Democratic officials and approved by everyone involved in the process. I saw the deadly serious charges of racial harassment as scurrilous since they were not backed by clear and solid evidence. I saw the mantra that Gore won the popular vote as diversionary since winning the popular vote in our system ranks along the lines of being Miss Congeniality at a beauty contest. Besides, neither of the candidates campaigned with a strategy to win the popular vote. In fact, when polls indicated that the vice president might lose the popular vote and win the electoral tally, the Gore camp noted such an eventuality should not be cause to question the legitimacy of the election. Yet when they were on the wrong side of the equation, they did a complete flip and stuck the landing.

Application

It is human nature to divert attention when arguments are not going the way we had hoped. Those with whom you discuss faith are going to use this technique with great acumen. Consider the following list of challenges; each point could be either a legitimate question or a diversion. You have probably heard most of them.

- How can a loving God allow such suffering in the world?
- Why is Jesus the only way to faith? Aren't all religions a pathway to heaven?
- What about all the hypocrites?
- The Bible is full of contradictions.
- Christianity draws on myths and legends.
- Science has proved that Creation is not a fact.

As a follower of Christ, you have to be sensitive to the person citing these objections. The challenge is to discern between legitimate concerns and diversions. I would suggest that you can often discern from people's attitudes whether they are honestly seeking answers or trying to bog you down with difficult questions. Understanding the tactic of diversion will help you to remain patient and focused. Reading some good apologetics books (*Mere Christianity* by C. S. Lewis or *Christianity for Skeptics* by Steve Kumar are two examples) will be helpful, but be honest and just admit it when you don't have all the answers.

Whether Christian or naturalist or atheist or nihilist, any position a person stakes out will ultimately rely upon faith. No honest person can claim with 100-percent assurance that he is right. So it is with Christianity. I believe that Christianity offers more of the answers to more of life's important questions. Even though faith is an undeniable component of Christianity, God provides sufficient evidence to those looking for it. Satan muddies the water enough to drive away folks who are merely looking for problems. I could argue the reliability of the biblical texts. I could present reams of evidence to support the historical accuracy of the Scriptures. I could mount a scientific argument for the possibility of intelligent design in creation that would at the very least gain the respect of skeptics. I could produce thousands upon thousands of anecdotal success stories from people of impeccable reputation and intelligence whose lives have been positively changed by faith in Christ. In short, I could build a case that would make Johnnie Cochran plea bargain, and it would still come down to faith on the part of the hearer.

When in doubt, we can tend to divert. Be discerning about the diversions. Be ready to address honest doubts and objections. But if you sense the questions are merely smoke screens to avoid confronting the question of faith, try to lovingly steer your challenger back to the most important question any of us will ever face: "Who is Jesus Christ and what does that mean to me?"

LESSON FIVE: WITHOUT A STANDARD, THERE IS NO BASIS FOR COMMUNICATION

As the deadline loomed concerning which ballots would count and which would not, the standards for evaluating the punch cards remained inconsistent. Proposed rules concerning the counting of "chads" sounded like Old Testament Levitical law:

"If the chad hangeth by one corner it shall be declared clean and shall count. If the chad hangeth by two corners it is clean and shall count. But if the chad is attached by three corners then it shall be unclean for you and will not count. But if, when the priest examines the chad, it is merely bulging, it shall be declared unclean and should not be counted."

What We All Saw

Chaos. Watching the footage from Palm Beach County showed what happens when standards are a moving target. One of the three-member panel decided to award votes to Vice President Gore if even a tiny indentation was noted in position number three. This was their ruling even if all other positions on the ballot were punched cleanly through. Well all righty then. So the fate of the free world comes down to a rerun of Carnac the Magnificent? Personally, I would hate to be judged by a jury with such subjective criteria.

Application

One of the arguments you will often hear from non-Christians is that God will weigh the good and bad in a person's life in determining his eternal home. If you have more good things than bad, you are in. If we can make counting a simple election ballot this complicated, I doubt that the average seeker really wants to roll the dice on how good works are counted toward salvation. Relativism may be maddening when counting chads, but the stakes are even higher when it comes to counting for eternity.

We have seen this kind of relativism flourish in recent years. There is a story told in *Christianity for Skeptics* about a college student who wrote a brilliantly researched paper arguing that there are no absolutes. He wrote persuasively and cogently that everything is relative. No paper was better documented or more scholarly. The professor returned the paper with a failing grade and a note attached saying, "I do not like blue covers." The student predictably went ballistic. He stormed into the professor's office and protested, "This isn't fair. I should be judged on the content of my paper!" The professor looked at the student and asked, "Was this the paper which argued there are no objective moral principles such as fairness and justice and everything is relative to one's taste?"

"Yes! Yes! That's the one."

"Well, then," the professor concluded. "I do not like blue covers. The grade will remain an F." And the student discovered the crack in his worldview foundation. He could argue the point that everything is relative, but *he expected* fairness to be applied to him.

Like the professor, we Christians must be prepared to point out the issues inherent in relativism. Every person (or at least anyone I want to be in the same zip code with) abides by some type of moral absolutes. Have you met any supporters of rape recently? How about those favoring child abuse? There are a large number of convicts serving time who feel those activities were "right" for them. So why are they incarcerated? Because we do believe that moral values exist.

Our pluralistic society considers it inflammatory to claim that Jesus is the only way to salvation. Folks run God through their American filter and decide that calling Jesus the only way to God isn't "fair." I simply tell them that I had to make a decision about God, about who He was and how He related to me. If God is God, I am not really in a strong position to dictate His program.

I am puzzled by the argument that God's rules just aren't fair. I hear statements like, "I can't worship a God who is so narrow-minded that there is only one way to get to heaven." Correct me if I am wrong, but can't God pretty much set any rules He likes? Whether we want to take our spiritual football and go home doesn't really matter. The question is simple. Is God who He said He is? If He is, then we can't go changing the rules like that six-year-old child playing board games or that forty-six-year-old official changing election rules. Isn't it more than a little bit ludicrous that we should suggest to the Creator of the Universe how He should run His business?

My editor fusses at me for having too many sports analogies, but I haven't spent the last twenty-five years directing television events for the Home & Garden Network. So here we go. Let's say that I was a football player for the Green Bay Packers in the 1960s. The coach was the legendary Vince Lombardi, a man considered by most to be one of the all-time great coaches. Coach Lombardi did things his way, and there was no other way to become a Packer except his way. He cared about his players, but if you chose another approach, you were choosing to be on another team. Imagine having this little dialogue with Coach Lombardi.

I approach Vince Lombardi with the following credentials: I'm a good guy but a lousy football player.

Me: Coach, I have a philosophical problem with the way you are doing things.

Vince: ?

Me: It really seems unfair to me that you are so narrow-minded about what it takes to be a Packer.

Vince: ?????

Me: You see, there are a lot of sincere and good football players who are trying their best to do the right thing here in training camp, and yet you demand they do it your way. That really doesn't seem fair to me. Do you feel that is right?

Vince: @#$%^&*(!@#$%^&*(

Me: I think that when training camp is over every single one of the boys who tried real hard and did more good things than bad things should be a Packer. I mean, how can you really care about your players if you are going to cut those guys who tried but won't do it your way? A really caring coach would let them all on the team. Whaddya think, Coach?

Me (on my rear end outside Vince's office): See, I told you he doesn't care about me. I can't follow a coach who isn't open-minded enough to look at other good, sincere football players and allow them to be Packers too.

Ridiculous? Yeah. We would never dream of trying to set the rules for someone as powerful and successful as Vince Lombardi. Yet we will argue about how God has no right to be restrictive on how you can come into His family? Again, it seems to me that we are asking all the wrong questions.

Christians get dismissed with condescending pats on our needy little heads with phrases like, "That is truth for you, but it isn't for me." There is an inherent problem with that statement. If it is truth, then it is truth for everyone. Jesus said some pretty outrageous things about how to have a relationship with God. You have the choice to accept Him as truth or reject Him as a liar. Don't patronize the man who claimed to be the Son of God. If Jesus was not telling the truth, he was not a "great teacher" and cannot be dismissed as such. Jesus is truth or He is not the truth. There are two options. Period.

LESSON SIX: PARTISANS MAKE THEIR POINTS WITH SELECTIVE PARTICULARS

What They Said

Immediately after Election Day, attorneys and operatives loudly proclaimed that the election was "stolen," as the Gore partisans declared the Palm Beach county ballot "patently illegal." According to Gore supporters, Florida election law requires standard paper ballots to list candidates in a specified order, with the check box to the right of each name. That is a fact. And it is a fact that Palm Beach did not follow these requirements. Sounds like an open-and-shut case. But they left out an inconvenient fact or two.

Additional Facts

Because Palm Beach County used machine-readable ballot cards, the rules for paper ballots do not apply. There is a separate provision in Florida law for the use of these cards. The Palm Beach ballots were entirely legal under this separate provision, but Gore supporters didn't mention that.

Many voters were undoubtedly confused even though most were able to figure it out. There may well have been a problem with the ballot. The ballot will probably need to be eliminated from any future use. But the ballot was not illegal. By using selective facts, the protesters were able to cast a more sinister tint to the issue. It was not emotional enough to say that there was an error in the ballot's design. The emotional hook was that the ballot was "illegal."

Application

We need to be cautious about using selective facts to try and generate an emotional response from the non-Christians we meet. Christians are especially good at getting part of a story and whipping up a big batch of embarrassing hype.

Last year I received an Internet forward from an acquaintance who believes anything sent on the Web must be true. The story was that some Siberian scientists were drilling a nine-mile-deep hole for reasons that were never quite clear. At some point the drill slipped and a hideous batlike creature flew out. Instead of heading back for a shot of vodka, they decided to lower a microphone into the mysterious hole. (Does the local Siberian Radio Shack carry nine-mile-long mike cords?) Anyway, according to this story, they heard and recorded tormented screams, and concluded that they had drilled to hell. This Internet link included an audio file of the screams that you could link to and listen. I have encountered sincere and caring Christians who share this story (and others like it) as a warning to come to faith in Christ. We don't need questionable facts to represent the gospel of Jesus Christ. We need to understand who Christ is, what that means to an individual both on a daily basis and into eternity, and then model those truths for those we encounter.

So, when discussing the faith with others, don't try to "win" every point by using partial or questionable information. If you don't know, say so. If you have doubts, say so. If you have struggled with something, say so. I still have unanswered questions about my faith and probably will until my death. Even so, I have received enough answers and I have had enough experiences to solidify my commitment to Christ. Be honest. God is in the process of drawing others to Himself, and you don't have to slam-dunk every objection to seal the deal.

In the book of Acts, Agrippa gave the apostle Paul permission to speak for himself which was all that Paul needed. He detailed his Damascus road experience and explained Christ's resurrection. Paul proclaimed that Jesus would be a light to His own people and to the Gentiles. This was enough for Festus, a member of the

King's court. "You are out of your mind, Paul!" he shouted. "Your great learning is driving you insane" (26:24). Paul was cool:

> "I am not insane, most excellent Festus. . . . What I am saying is true and reasonable. The king is familiar with these things, and I can speak freely to him. I am convinced that none of this has escaped his notice, because it was not done in a corner. King Agrippa, do you believe the prophets? I know you do."
>
> Then Agrippa said to Paul, "Do you think that in such a short time you can persuade me to be a Christian?"
>
> Paul replied, "Short time or long—I pray God that not only you but all who are listening to me today may become what I am, except for these chains" (26:25-29)

Every Christian has to answer for his or her motives when seeking to bring others to faith. I pray that I am not arrogant in my desire. I hope I am not proud. I believe what I espouse is true and reasonable. I have discovered a faith that works. I have no huge agenda. That is how I view faith in Christ. I have joy. I have peace. I want others to have the same. That's as complicated as it gets for this writer.

Chapter 13

Don't Know Much About Theology

Genius may have its limitations, but stupidity is not thus handicapped.

—ELBERT HUBBARD

The Michigan Lawsuit Abuse Watch organization sponsors an annual contest for the most ridiculous warning label on consumer products. Here is just a sampling of the warnings that manufacturers apparently feel we need:

- A warning label found on a baby stroller cautions the user to "Remove child before folding."
- A household iron warns users: "Never iron clothes while they are being worn."
- A thirteen-inch wheel on a wheelbarrow warns: "Not intended for highway use."
- A warning on an electric router (made for carpenters) cautions: "This product not intended for use as a dental drill."

Perhaps the most frightening aspect of these labels is that there was some perceived reason to find them necessary.

Sam Cooke had a hit song in the '60s called "Wonderful World." The lyrics ("Don't know much about...") always made me laugh as this clever guy touted his lack of academic achievement in order to win his girl's love. I loved that song. Anyone who could parlay being a complete academic slacker into a romantic strength could be on my team.

WELL, WHAT DO YOU KNOW?

The Christian community is not immune to occasional spiritual dimness. My ode to our own intellectual shortcomings, with apologies to the late Sam Cooke, might go something like this:

> Don't know much about theology,
> Don't know much Christology.
> Don't know much about Leviticus,
> Don't know why they had the Exodus.
> But I do know that God loves you,
> And I'm trying hard to be good too.
> What a wonderful faith this would be.
>
> Well, I don't claim to be a good Christian,
> But I'm trying to be.
> For maybe by bein' a good person, brother,
> I can gain eternity.
>
> (Everyone now...)

Don't know much about the Pharisees,
Can't explain the Trinity.
Don't know much ecclesiology
Don't know what a good tithe should be.
But I think that God forgives my quirks,
And I figure if I do good works,
What a wonderful faith this would be.

Putting spiritual ignorance to music might be amusing, but the issue is serious. Speaking for myself, if I exercised the same work ethic with my job that I have with my faith, I would be scouring want ads. Many of us take little or no time to learn the basics of our faith, and then we wonder why it isn't working. In many cases it isn't working because we haven't read the instructions.

A frequent Internet forward is a list of the World's Thinnest or Skinniest Books. You have probably seen a variation of the list that includes such skinny classics as:

- *My Favorite Spotted Owl Recipes* by Al Gore
- *The Amish Big Book of Technology*
- *Things I Can't Afford* by Bill Gates
- *My Plan to Find the Real Killers* by O. J. Simpson

We could add our own very thin Christian books to the list:

- *The Southern Baptist Guide to Disney World*
- *The Assemblies of God Cocktail Mix Guide*
- *Things I Have No Opinion About* by Pat Robertson
- *Benny Hinn's Documented Healings*
- *Living a Sacrificial Lifestyle* by Robert Tilton

The saddest and most serious thin-book title that we might see is *Christian Doctrine I Am Sure Is True.* According to the always thought-provoking researcher George Barna, the average Christian possesses a shallow grasp of evangelical Christian doctrine. In a Barna survey of more than one thousand Christian adults, 90 percent stated that they were very familiar with the teachings of Christianity. If their responses are proof of familiarity with Christian teachings, then I am tempted to say I am very familiar with quantum physics because I can spell it without the aid of spell check.

Here is a sampling of what Barna found these Christian adults said they believe from the online report *Americans' Bible Knowledge Is in the Ballpark, But Often Off Base,* July 12, 2000 (http://www.barna.org). I have combined the respondents' percentages for those who agreed strongly and agreed somewhat to reach the numbers below.

- 58 percent believed the devil is just a symbol.
- 39 percent thought Jesus was human and committed sins.
- 61 percent think the Holy Spirit is a symbol and not a living entity.
- 75 percent believe that God helps those who help themselves.
- Only 60 percent think the Bible is totally accurate in all that it teaches.
- 44 percent of Christians think it doesn't matter what religion you follow.

I was stunned. If this is representative (and Mr. Barna has a pretty good track record), then it is small wonder that the church has been ineffectual and that Christians demonstrate little distinction from unbelievers in their day-to-day lives. Of the 1,003 adults Barna interviewed, only three (yes, that's three!) demonstrated a firm and biblically consistent position on all fourteen of the doctrinal statements that he surveyed. That number again, folks, is *three*—an incredible .00299 percent! I'm not talking about doctrinal positions that we can honestly debate. The statements that comprised the survey pertained to the fundamentals of the faith. Perhaps we should have a little doctrinal boot camp before we start worrying about whether we should be allowed to display the Ten Commandments in courtrooms. (By the way, a Gallup poll found that six in ten Americans couldn't name half of the Ten Commandments and couldn't even begin to put them in order.)

So what's the big deal? Do we really need to be theological experts to live the Christian life? Well, I would submit that we usually take the time to learn the benefits of far less important aspects of our lives. For followers of Jesus, our faith in Him is (or should be) the most important thing in our lives. It should be more important than the stock market. More important than *Sports Center.* More important than our work. Our faith is the foundation of everything we do. Our faith and doctrine define the worldview that influences our marriage, family, child raising, personal morality, and ethics. It is no surprise that so many Christians possess confused worldviews; our foundational beliefs are equally confused.

I'm a member of a national auto club. I claim to be affiliated with this auto club. But my membership would be of little or no value to me if I had no idea what benefits it offered. Suppose I have a breakdown on a remote stretch of highway. The club offers free emergency roadside service that I could access from my cell phone. Instead I choose to walk ten miles to the nearest exit. The auto club offers free towing to get my car to a service facility. But I decide to call an unrelated towing company and pay for towing costs out of my own pocket. When I get back on the road, I pull into a hotel and pay the highest rate, even though my membership in the auto club entitles me to a nice discount. After leaving the hotel I get lost and then delayed in construction zones despite the auto club's service that provides directions and up-to-date construction alerts. You would think I am a moron for not being informed and not utilizing the benefits of being a member of the auto club.

That, far more tragically, is what millions of us do as members of the body of Christ. We don't comprehend the basic truths of what we believe and therefore cannot implement those truths in our daily lives.

Returning to the Barna Institute research, let's revisit the sad list from above. Well over half of Christians surveyed believe the devil is just a symbol. No wonder we so are often unprepared for spiritual warfare. Evil is not just symbolic. The influence of the devil and of evil is very real. Those who deal regularly in the dark underworld of society will tell you that there is more than just lack of opportunity or education behind many of the crimes and acts of hatred they see. There is evil in this world. We are not evolving into better creatures. If you don't believe me, sit down and talk to any big-city cop or detective. They will tell you of the skin-crawling presence of evil that they feel when they are near some of these frightening people.

Christians must acknowledge the real presence of the devil and evil. In Mark's gospel Jesus Himself was directly tempted by Satan to sin. In his letter to the Ephesians, the apostle Paul outlined how we can defend ourselves against the forces of evil. We can hardly dismiss the presence of evil when it is so prominently discussed in

Scripture. Ephesians 6:11-13 tells us: "Put on the full armor of God so that you can take your stand against the devil's schemes. For our struggle is not against flesh and blood, but against the rulers, against the authorities, against the powers of this dark world and against the spiritual forces of evil in the heavenly realms. Therefore put on the full armor of God, so that when the day of evil comes, you may be able to stand your ground, and after you have done everything, to stand."

Amazingly, over 80 percent of these same Barna respondents believed in the presence of angels. Scripture does not allow you to believe in the good (angels) and reject the bad (Satan and the forces of evil). The fact that Satan is a fallen angel makes it even more difficult to believe only in the presence of angels. Author Wade Clark Roof calls our pick-and-choose mentality the "spiritual quest culture." Boomers believe that life is a spiritual journey to try and find truth for "me." Sounds like a few strands of relativism are being woven into our theological tapestry. He also points out how people are reluctant to be called "religious" now (all that intolerance and ignorance, you know); we like to be called "spiritual" ("Oh, I don't go to church, but I'm a very 'spiritual' person"). Being a "spiritual" person is nice, but it doesn't automatically answer the important questions that each of us must answer.

That such a high percentage of Christian adults think that Jesus was merely human and committed sins is especially distressing. Nearly one-third believed that Jesus died but did not have a physical resurrection. That negates the very essence of Jesus and who He said He was. If Jesus was merely human, committed sin, and did not have a bodily resurrection, then Christianity is truly no different from any other religion.

And perhaps the biggest indicator of why so many of us don't experience more joy in our Christian walk is the percentage of Christians who believe the Holy Spirit, like the devil, is merely a symbol and not a living being. The essence of being able to live any kind of a successful Christian life is understanding and appropriating the comfort and direction of the Holy Spirit.

THE PROBLEM WITH ILLITERACY

George Barna is not the only one who has pointed out the torpidity of the average Christian when it comes to biblical literacy. Studies show that a little over 90 percent of Americans own a Bible, but it appears that far too many of us are using them as doorstops or paperweights. A Gallup survey reported that fewer than half of Americans can name the first book of the Bible. Only one-third correctly named Jesus as the source of the Sermon on the Mount. (Several named Billy Graham as the one who delivered that message.) George W. Gallup correctly observed that "we revere the Bible but we don't read it."

I have a recurring nightmare of dying and going to heaven (that isn't the nightmare part). While strolling the streets, I bump into Obadiah. We discuss writing. "Did you read my book?" Obadiah asks expectantly.

"Book?" I say, looking puzzled.

"Old Testament! Right after Amos!" he says with as much anger as you are allowed in heaven.

"Oh. That one," I mumble. You don't want to have that kind of embarrassing encounter in paradise, trust me.

In an article for *Books and Culture,* Pastor Mark Buchanan

writes about the mishmash that we Boomers call doctrine. Buchanan writes: "[Boomers] want human closeness without feeling cramped or obligated. They want a personal God who doesn't ask much personally. They want mystery, but in a controlled, nondisruptive way. They want a faith that's fulfilling, practical, earthy, tolerant, transcendent, fun, empowering, morally serious without being morally demanding, a faith that restores wonder and deepens intimacy, and they want it *not to cost too much or take up a lot of time.*"

Just like the people in beer and investment commercials on television, we Christians want it all. How shallow and diminishing to our Savior to have such an egocentric belief system.

A Tyndale House Publishers survey revealed that 64 percent of Americans don't read the Bible because they are too busy. Again, if our faith is important, we will make the time. Not having enough time is a comforting rationalization until you decide to be honest with yourself. Time is a currency. You spend it on what is important to you. One of my core beliefs is that the investment of your time (over a long period) is a pretty accurate indicator of your priorities and actual loves. Let me add a disclaimer that I realize short-term financial, work, health, or other situations can temporarily rearrange priorities and time investments. But over the long haul, we can determine a great deal about our true loves through our time management. If I claim to love my children but make little or no time for them, then my claim rings hollow.

George Barna also noted that born-again adults spend an average of seven times more hours each week watching television than they do in spiritual pursuits (Bible reading, worship, prayer). He reported that they spend roughly twice as much money on entertainment as they donate to their local church. At this point in reading the report, my Pharisee pride began to puff up. I don't watch a lot of television and I'm not a big entertainment spender. I was thinking how glad I am that I'm not like those "other sinners." But then Barna continued.

Born-again Christians also spend more time surfing the Internet than they do conversing with God in prayer. Wait a minute. That's not fair. Suddenly I didn't care as much about Barna and his meddling research. A gentle nudging of the Spirit also reminded me that I spend more time on average studying the sports page than I do studying the Bible. "But sports is my career," my wounded pride called out. "I have to know what is going on in order to do my job." The gentle nudging continued. "Of course you do. But you are writing about priorities of time. About spending it on your real love. Where do you spend your time?"

Busted. I am truly embarrassed to report that I can name every starter from the 1961 Cincinnati Reds but would struggle to name all twelve disciples.

You make time for what is important. When I first fell in love with my wife, she was in my thoughts nearly all the time. I wanted to see her, talk to her, be near her, and share my every thought with her. Then I slowly fell in love with success in my career. I still loved my wife, but my time and priorities brutally indicated that my lust (a better word) for success was more important to me than she was. If I take this job or that trip, I will be on my way. Success is just around the corner. Then it was the next corner and so on and so on. My wife patiently (and occasionally not so patiently) waited and prayed for my priorities to change. They finally began to change, but not until after a series of painful wake-up calls.

Trust me, I am not antisuccess. I am not anticareer. Once, when

I was talking with a young married man about the need to prioritize time with his family, he replied, "That's easy for you to say. You have been successful and made your money." You can see the seductress Success claiming another victim.

What I have become is pro-balance. Seek the Lord's balance in career versus family. It is achievable. Seek a balance in your personal time. Jesus' life showed that balance. He often attended wedding feasts and parties. He spent time in fellowship with the Twelve. But he obviously balanced those times with time spent in prayer and reflection.

So many Christians have become totally out of balance. I would suggest keeping a time log for a couple of weeks. Just be honest. Or go back and look at your calendar last week. How did you spend your time? How much time did you spend talking with your spouse? How much individual time with each of your children? How much time with God in prayer or Bible reading? You might want to do a little rearranging of your time investments. I have begun to view my time like a mutual fund or investment portfolio. A good investment portfolio offers protection in various economic situations. One investment might do well when interest is high. Another when interest rates are down. You have something to fall back on no matter what the situation. The same strategy can be used for your time portfolio. Time invested in Bible reading and study will return rewards now and into eternity. Time spent with the wife will increase intimacy and give you a wise sounding board for your thoughts and ideas. Time invested in your children will return more than any stock ever could.

Perhaps the most frightening statistic of all is the 90 percent of Christians who believe they are knowledgeable about their faith.

When people think they know something (for example, men and directions) they are very unlikely to see the need to improve. Seventy-five percent of surveyed believers think that the Bible says that God helps those who help themselves. That quote probably first occurred in "Discourses on Government" by Sidney Algernon (1622–1683), but many attribute it to Ben Franklin. At any rate, it doesn't appear in the Bible. God is much more able to help those who can't help themselves, but Sidney's (or Ben's) take on this subject works a lot better with our culture. We like to be in charge. Brokenness shows weakness, and we can't admit that in this culture of self-sufficiency.

When you begin to comprehend what the research means, it becomes a little clearer why we are not impacting our culture. Far too many Christians don't know what they believe and what that lack of knowledge means to their daily activities. An unacceptable number of people who say they believe in Christ have no idea how to implement the power and benefit of that relationship with Jesus in their lives.

So we have a crisis here. We must get back to basics. There is really no good excuse not to know the fundamentals of faith. Imagine the same dynamic in other areas. What if you knew little to nothing about your college major after fifteen years of university attendance?

What if, after several years on the job, you had learned just bits and pieces about the intricacies of what you should be doing? That would be unacceptable to your employer. I am proposing (present company solidly included) that a lack of biblical and doctrinal fundamental knowledge is likewise unacceptable.

If we don't know what we believe, it is more than a little tough to bring others on board. Evangelism may be moribund because we don't know what to say to others. You can't explain what you don't know.

Also, when we lack a contextual understanding of the Bible, we can cherry pick verses to support just about anything. And over the years, people identifying themselves as Christians have used isolated Scripture verses to condone slavery, persecute Jews, discriminate against blacks, restrict women's rights, and justify hatred of homosexuals. The infamous Ku Klux Klan had an opening and closing prayer that included the incredible claim that "The living Christ is a Klansman's criterion of character." I would laugh if it weren't so tragic. The living Christ is the antithesis of the Klan, and knowledge of the totality of the Bible would lead a Klansman to either leave or know that he was willfully disobeying God's Word. As for homosexuality, the Bible does say in the Old Testament that it is an abomination to God. But don't forget the other abominations listed. Adultery. Sex outside of marriage. Killing innocents (abortion?). Lying. Lust. Prostitution. Disobedience. Oppression of the poor. Pride. Spreading discord. According to Levitical law, adultery was to be punished by stoning. Ready for that to go back into effect? The Bible must be viewed in its total context, and verse roulette is not the way to build a biblical position. The Old Testament must be integrated with the New Covenant of Christ.

Suppose I picked up a rule book for a game and built my entire competition around one rule that supported my particular competitive strength. You would think I was crazy. You would no doubt scream at me that the entire rule book must come into play if I want to understand the game. It is the same with God's rule book. Ignorance is not bliss when it comes to the spiritual issues we address. The prophet Hosea proclaimed "my people are destroyed from lack of knowledge" (4:6). He could be speaking to the body of Christ today.

Without a working knowledge of the faith, we tend to be blended believers. We throw everything from New Age to relativism to traditional Protestantism to Americanism into the blender and hit "purée." What we get may or may not be Christianity, but we don't seem to mind as long as it goes down smoothly.

This neutered faith we have concocted is little, if at all, different from other religions. Isn't it interesting: Those of us whose lives have been changed by Jesus probably originally embraced Christianity in the first place *because* it was different! It offered us a relationship with a living God, not a religion based on impossible rules and laws.

We must do a better job of knowing what we believe and the biblical basis for it, not just what we heard somewhere from someone. Dorothy Sayers framed the issue well when she wrote, "The proper question to be asked about any creed is not 'Is it pleasant?' but 'Is it true?'" Without the Bible, we have no checkpoint for evaluating the influx of ideas. No plumb line of truth to measure information.

In John 4, Jesus talked to the woman at the well about drinking the "living water" that would satisfy thirst forever. Our theological and biblical ignorance has left much of the body of Christ severely dehydrated and feeling spiritually weakened. If you are feeling a little thirsty, the fountain is flowing freely. But you have to go there to drink. And often.

Chapter 14

All God's Children Got Souls, Even the Annoying Ones

I like long walks, especially when they are taken by people who annoy me.

—NOEL COWARD

C ome on…admit it. Some people you just don't like. If you are like me, it is really difficult to care about their salvation. It is burdensome, if not impossible, to pray for them. But the truth is that all of God's children got souls, even the annoying ones. That is a most difficult concept for me. My nature is more inclined to echo Mr. Coward's feelings above and to encourage all of you annoying folks to take long walks.

I confess that this is really a major personal issue. The world is full of people who annoy me! It is difficult for me to face up to my responsibilities to be an ambassador for Jesus Christ. I would prefer to be in the Witness Protection program.

IRRITATING BUT TRUE

Ted Turner drew uproars from the Christian community when he said, "Christianity is a religion for losers." Many Christian leaders got their BVDs all bunched up and announced how much Captain Outrageous offended them.

Let me suggest an idea for my Christian brethren to consider. (For the record, I do not open my own mail. It is sent to a warehouse and opened by robots.) Let's assume, just for the sake of argument, that many of the Christians Mr. Turner has encountered were in fact, uh, losers.

Those of us already in the club know that on certain days we would prefer not to have someone's evaluation of Jesus resting on our performance as His representative. After all, living the Christian life is a little like golf. Just when you think you have it all figured out, you have the worst round of your life. I know all too well that I've had days when people who come into contact with me would consider me a "loser" for the way I portray my faith. On other days they would find me kind and caring and concerned. On some days the swing is smooth, and I am hitting fairways and rolling in my putts. The next round I am in the woods, breaking clubs and using language that might require parental guidance (you know…like "dadgum" and "Godfrey Daniels"). If Ted Turner observed me on that day, he would be arguably correct in calling me a loser for claiming a life-changing belief in Christ and living a life that hardly reflects that.

"But everyone makes mistakes," you protest. "Everyone is a sinner who must rely on the unbelievable grace of the Lord." Bingo. You know that. I know that. Bob Dole knows that. But just maybe Ted Turner doesn't know that. Maybe he has been terribly hurt by Christians somewhere along the way. In fact, at a United Nations Peace Summit, Mr. Turner once denounced his childhood faith and called it "intolerant." Interesting, isn't it: By excoriating him, we confirm his beliefs that Christians are intolerant. The uproar from the church actually proves his point. If I am solidly aligned with the Savior of the world, however, Ted Turner's opinion really doesn't carry any weight, and I certainly shouldn't be threatened by it.

Minnesota Governor Jesse Ventura likewise stirred up the flock by saying, "Organized religion is a sham and a crutch for weak-minded people who need strength in numbers." I would have to say that a disturbingly high percentage of organized religion has been a sham. Note that I said "organized religion," which bears little resemblance to genuine Christianity. Groups and denominations that have claimed affiliation with Christ and not followed His teachings are a sham and have, in fact, been dangerous. (I have to admit that I recoil a bit at the "weak-minded" reference, but it is a conviction of mine that I will not be intimidated by men who wear feather boas.) As with Mr. Turner, I must wonder whether Mr. Ventura has really known a sincere, dedicated, and sold-out follower of Christ. You may call such a person a lot of things, but "weak-minded" does not come to mind when you examine the selfless service of faithful Christians around the world.

Shock-rocker Marilyn Manson loves to denigrate Christianity. It is common to see Christian groups picketing outside his concerts. His lyrics are crude, vulgar, angry, and far too graphic to sample here. Christian organizations have circulated false allegations about his antics (as if we couldn't find enough true stuff that was repulsive). But did you know that Mr. Manson attended a Christian school in Canton, Ohio, as Brian Warner? He was an awkward and self-described unattractive kid with few, if any, friends. In an interview with *Talk Magazine,* Manson said, "There is no support group for kids like this." Read Frank Peretti's painfully personal book *The Wounded Spirit* about his experience as a bullied and tormented student. Then consider how the scars of alienation can be manifested in either the angry music of Marilyn Manson or the Christ-honoring books of Frank Peretti. I think Peretti would tell you the difference was his support group: his church, his Christian family, and his friends. Where was the church when Brian Warner needed acceptance? And can anyone think that a calling to teach in public schools is not a ministry of the highest order? Not necessarily to proselytize, but just to be someone who cares for those whom no one else will. As Saint Francis of Assisi so wonderfully observed, "Preach the gospel at all times. If necessary, use words."

In the interview, Mr. Manson went on to say, "There is no one marching in front of the Democratic convention saying, 'What about the pimply-faced white teenager who gets beat up at school every day?' That's what I was. There was no one there to stick up for me."

Tragically for Brian Warner, we instinctively move to march against lyrics instead of being available for the kids who gravitate toward them in the first place. Maybe we can't save them all, but we can save some from the feelings of utter despair and alienation that Manson felt.

MOVING IN A NEW DIRECTION

It is easier to be critical than truly helpful. In the gospel of John, Jesus talked about how we must be in relationship with Him before we can be fruitful in our daily endeavors. Bruce Wilkinson's book *Secrets of the Vine* outlines the intricate relationships of the vine and fruit reflected in the parable. But simply stated, when you are in a vital relationship with Christ, your thoughts and actions will reflect that connection.

> Remain in me, and I will remain in you. No branch
> can bear fruit by itself; it must remain in the vine.
> Neither can you bear fruit unless you remain in me.
> I am the vine; you are the branches. If a man
> remains in me and I in him, he will bear much
> fruit; apart from me you can do nothing. If anyone
> does not remain in me, he is like a branch that is
> thrown away and withers; such branches are picked
> up, thrown into the fire and burned. (John 15:4-6)

We must be connected to the Vine to produce the fruit that God desires. I can tell you that when my entire crop is sour grapes, I am not grafted properly to the Vine. This means that I'm not consistent in having the maturity or the heart attitude to see each person as a precious soul in His eyes. When I get on an airplane, I typically don't want to talk to the person next to me. If I ask how he or she is doing, I don't always really want to know. Spending the emotional energy to care about someone requires a commitment, and I am often too selfish to make that commitment to a person I may never see again.

Yet serving others is often simply a matter of being responsive to the Holy Spirit's prompting. Joni and I have an answering machine that emits a gentle beep when there is a message. When the house is noisy, I don't hear the gentle ping, ping, ping that indicates a message. God speaks to my heart with a similar gentle signal. I have to slow down and be quiet long enough to hear the spiritual ping.

So what is the key to becoming more effective in service? For me it is the simple concept of baby steps. I am not going to be where I want to be in just six weeks or after a twenty-one-step program or a three-point sermon. When I view where I am versus where I would like to be, I get discouraged. The old concept that the journey of a thousand miles starts with the first step rings true with Christian growth. If I want to run a marathon, I must take certain actions to accomplish my goal. If I only talk about running a marathon, I will last about half a mile. If I go to seminars and absorb wisdom from the top runners in the world, I will still last about a half-mile. If I study the best journals about running and learn everything there is to know about kinesiology, I will get about a half-mile into the race. Running a marathon involves getting up, getting out, and getting started. The first run may be only a few yards. Then you can run a mile, a couple of miles, then five, ten and so on. It's a marathon, and you can't will yourself through discipline or even faith to finish without taking small steps first. There is no other way to go about it. (Lest anyone get confused, I am not advocating a works theology. I am advocating that growing in the faith does involve getting over the sin of inertia and getting the derrière moving.)

Don't worry about the size of the commitment. I have learned that when you venture out and do something, the rewards keep taking you back to it. The concept of receiving more than you give is never truer than when you serve others for Christ.

I recently made a commitment to be more patient with those dearly beloved idiots I encounter in the daily rush. Sure enough, opportunity knocked quickly. At the grand opening of a local store, the parking lot was packed. As I circled, I noticed a car backing out. I felt quite lucky as I pulled in and locked the car to go inside. As I left my car I noticed a man in a gigantic SUV waiting behind me and glowering. "Thanks a lot!" he grumbled at me. "I was waiting for that spot." At first I was flustered. I honestly did not realize that he was waiting, but my first reaction was the familiar testosterone territorial-anger flush. Then my commitment flashed through my mind.

"I'm very sorry," I said. "I had no idea you were waiting. Please back up and I will give you this spot." Now it was his turn to be a little taken aback.

"No, no," harrumphed the driver. "Forget it!" (I have been waiting forty years to be able to use *harrumph* in an illustration.)

"I'm serious," I said. "I did not mean to take your spot. Please take it." He slowly started to back up his land yacht. As I got in my car, I turned and said, "Sorry again. God bless you." You should have seen the look on his face. Later in the day I would recall that look and smile. After I backed out and gave up the spot another space opened up literally forty feet further away (I consider it my personal mini–Red Sea experience).

So what where the results of my baby step toward being kinder? I kept my blood pressure down. I may have given the man a reason to be a little kinder next time. My parting comment may have caused him to think. But the bottom line is *I just felt better.* I knew I had done the right thing as an act of obedience to God, and it felt good. You really should have seen the guy's face.

STRENGTH IN OBEDIENCE

I wonder if you experienced an involuntary recoil when you read the word *obedience* above. Boy, does the concept of obedience cut to the "me" core of our culture. "I ain't gonna be obedient or grammatically correct for nobody!" we shout. But I would argue that obedience is another word that has been culturally debased. *Obedient* means "willing to follow the directions of one in authority." We have made it instead to mean docile, weak, and without conviction or strength. Kind of a lap dog. Obedience to God is anything but weak, and it often requires more conviction and strength than all of your critics combined could muster. Dietrich Bonhoeffer wrote, "One act of obedience is better than one hundred sermons." And if you know much about Bonhoeffer, you know that he was a man of great conviction and strength who ultimately gave his life for his faith.

I experienced the joy of obedience on a mundane plane flight. I tell you the following story not to pat myself on the back but to point out how God can bless you when you are simply available to serve. I was traveling back home to Dallas from Fayetteville, Arkansas, after a college basketball game. While waiting to board the plane, I noticed a little boy who was obviously going through chemotherapy, his bald head covered with a baseball cap. My heart did go out to him and his parents, but I went back to reading the paper and getting ready for my flight.

Then it was announced that our flight was canceled. I went upstairs to the ticket line, but that queue was dozens of people deep. So I picked up my cell phone, called the frequent flyer desk, and reworked my reservation over the phone. Then I noticed the little boy and his family behind me. They seemed a little distraught. I asked them if I could help, and I found out his story.

Little Jacob was going to Orlando to take a Disney Cruise courtesy of the Make-a-Wish Foundation, the wonderful charity that fulfills the desires of terminal or seriously ill children. He was going to miss his connection, and the family was obviously concerned. I called the frequent flyer desk for Delta and explained the situation. The representative graciously rebooked Jacob and his family on a later connection that would still get him there on time. Now we had to get him out of Fayetteville. The next flight was overbooked, and Jacob and his family would have to go standby. If he missed that flight, then they would still have difficulties getting to Orlando on time. So I told them I would give up my seat to them. Then I recruited some other people who also gave up their seats so Jacob and his parents could get to Disney World.

I felt pretty good about helping out. But it got better. Little Jacob walked over to me and stood in front of me, looking right into my face as only little children can do. I smiled at him and started to make small talk when he stepped forward and threw his arms around my neck and hugged me. Tears welled in my cynical eyes as I held that fragile and precious little guy.

As it turned out, all of us got on the flight. Several people quietly slipped money to Jacob's parents, including one lady who handed the family a one-hundred-dollar bill for their trip. None of us felt put out. All of us were blessed by being able to help him.

And that is the lesson of service that Satan does not want us to experience. When you give, you do receive. Max Lucado says, "We are at our best when we are giving. In fact, we are most like God when we are giving." I drove home after the flight thanking God for the opportunity to show His love. At the same time, I wondered how many times I have missed the chance to help because I was all wrapped up in me. I have contemplated instituting the Copernicus Award to give to those who think that they are the center of the universe and that the entire universe revolves around their needs. The truth is, I would be among the most consistent recipients.

Jacob wasn't a difficult person to love. The real rub as a Christian comes in caring about those who aren't so easy to feel compassion or love for. I was saddened to read about a Christian homeless shelter that refused to let a gay man serve at the Thanksgiving dinner because his beliefs were "inconsistent" with their beliefs. The spokesman went on to say, "We wouldn't want anyone who advocated adultery to serve either." That comment triggered my recall of something Jesus once said in response to a similar issue.

> When a woman who had lived a sinful life in that
> town learned that Jesus was eating at the Pharisee's
> house, she brought an alabaster jar of perfume, and
> as she stood behind him at his feet weeping, she
> began to wet his feet with her tears. Then she wiped
> them with her hair, kissed them and poured per-
> fume on them.
>
> When the Pharisee who had invited him saw
> this, he said to himself, "If this man were a prophet,

he would know who is touching him and what kind
of woman she is—that she is a sinner."

Jesus answered him, "Simon, I have something
to tell you."

"Tell me, teacher," he said.

"Two men owed money to a certain money-
lender. One owed him five hundred denarii, and
the other fifty. Neither of them had the money to
pay him back, so he canceled the debts of both.
Now which of them will love him more?"

Simon replied, "I suppose the one who had the
bigger debt canceled."

"You have judged correctly," Jesus said.

Then he turned toward the woman and said to
Simon, "Do you see this woman? I came into your
house. You did not give me any water for my feet,
but she wet my feet with her tears and wiped them
with her hair. You did not give me a kiss, but this
woman, from the time I entered, has not stopped
kissing my feet. You did not put oil on my head,
but she has poured perfume on my feet. Therefore,
I tell you, her many sins have been forgiven—for
she loved much. But he who has been forgiven little
loves little." (Luke 7:37-47)

Jesus not only allowed the sinful woman to "serve," but He
saw in her a heart attitude that shamed those around her.

I have started trying to see every person as having value in
God's eyes. When someone cuts me off in traffic, I think that

Christ died for that person. When people irritate me or are rude, I try to think that they were created in the image of God and they just need a little image makeover at this moment. When I engage in people-watching, I try to breathe a prayer for them instead of critiquing their clothing. I do not always pull this off, but the discipline has begun to change how I view people. It is not easy to consistently view others through the lens of Jesus' love. But ultimately the Spirit will remind me, and my attitude toward the person in question is inevitably changed.

It's no wonder that grace and forgiveness are the rarest of commodities in this society. Oscar Wilde said, "Always forgive your enemies; nothing annoys them so much." Actually, nothing disarms them so much because forgiveness is not a natural act.

We are to be light in a world whose soul seems to get a little darker everyday. What does that mean? I have not had success sharing my faith via a clever T-shirt or Christian tie. And wielding a blinding searchlight seeking sin and sinners has, inexplicably, been ineffective. My moments of pompous moralizing have not brought converts racing to the flock.

What does it mean then, to be a light in the darkness? Many of us are, in reality, rheostat Christians. For those of you not as handy around the house as I am (a laugh line just for my wife), a rheostat is a switch that allows you to control the amount of electrical current. Simply stated, the rheostat on a lamp functions as a dimmer. You can dim the lights or go to full brightness depending on the situation. I tend to operate like a rheostat believer. If I am in a comfortable situation, I turn up my Christian rheostat to full brightness. I say tidy Christian things and act very Christian. But if the environment is hostile or intellectually uncomfortable, I am tempted and sometimes intimidated into turning the dimmer to low or to no light at all.

I think Christ would have us replace the rheostat with a motion detector switch. When a person comes into your path, the light comes on and stays on. I'm not saying that you attack them with the gospel. Just be real and available. When we become confident in our faith we'll begin to develop an ever-greater ability to be consistent.

I can tell non-Christians what I have experienced and learned about the gospel of Jesus Christ. But before I can tell them about Christ, I have to care about them. Mother Teresa was quoted as saying that the "greatest suffering is to be unwanted, unloved, uncared for, to be shunned by everyone, to be just nobody." We can make a difference to some of the hurting souls who feel like that. So when it comes to all those annoying people, my prayer is to have the spiritual equivalent of Michelangelo's artistic vision. The great sculptor proclaimed, "I saw the angel in the marble and carved until I set him free." May God give us the desire and vision to see the beauty of the soul in the sinner and love them until God sets them free.

Chapter 15

Pleading Humanity

*What lies behind us and what lies before us are tiny matters
compared to what lies within us.*

—RALPH WALDO EMERSON

History records that approximately a hundred different "messiahs" were running around during the time of Christ. It is possible that some of them had followers as impressive as the twelve selected by Jesus. Jesus took twelve guys of questionable attributes and built the largest faith in the world.

Not one of the other would-be messiahs' influence made it into the second century, let alone the twenty-first. So our calendar is dated by the birth of Christ. Does it not pique your curiosity that such a band of men could have such a global impact? No other man in history has had a greater effect, yet His ministry lasted only three years and ended in betrayal and a criminal execution. His blue-collar band of disciples led a religion that turned the world upside down. His disciples scattered and, on the way out the door, denied Him. And yet something transformed them, and they later had the courage to stand against persecution and even death to proclaim His truth. Somehow these men were persuasive enough to influence people to spread His gospel all over the globe.

Does it not seem odd that the leaders of that day who possessed absolute power could not stamp out this modest little faith? Why did they not produce the body of Jesus and put an end to the craziness once and for all? It was certainly in the best interests of Rome and the comfortable "Religious Right" of the day to quell this peasant uprising. Or, if they couldn't produce the body, why didn't they simply discredit the Resurrection account in such a way that no one would believe it? The resurrection of Christ is a pretty outrageous claim, and it would seem easy to refute. Yet they didn't, and apparently they couldn't.

Imagine the odds today of taking eleven working men from a blue-collar setting, adding a CPA to the ranks, and starting a religion under an oppressive government. The accomplishments of Jesus' ragamuffin group of men are unparalleled. They changed history. How could such a group do that?

LET'S START A REVOLUTION

First and foremost, Jesus was a total revolutionary. He granted status to women where none existed in the culture. His views were strange and upsetting to those in power. G. K. Chesterton decided that Jesus' views on marriage were "neither a product of His culture [n]or even a logical development from the time period. It is an utterly strange and wonderful teaching which bears the stigma of being from another world." In that period of history, women were viewed as property. Divorce was a no-fault procedure for the husband only. A wife could be dismissed for no reason and abandoned to great hardship and suffering; an abandoned wife had virtually no viable options for survival. And infanticide of baby girls was common in the Roman and pagan cultures. The early church did not condone or carry out this despicable practice.

The early church championed the concept of community responsibility. Professor Rodney Stark, in his fine book *The Rise of Christianity*, studied the early church and found that unbelievers were often attracted to the faith because of the tangible benefits provided by the charitable, care-giving Christians. Early Christian scribe Tertullian wrote late in the second century that pagan temples spent their donations on "feasts and drinking bouts." Donations of the Christians were used to "support and bury poor people, to supply the wants of boys and girls destitute of means and parents, and of old persons confined to the house." The pagan emperor Julian was amazed and even cynical when he noted, "The impious Galileans support not only their poor, but ours as well." That's quite a shot across the bow, isn't it? They act Christian at home and away! How dare they!

Professor E. Glenn Hinson writes, "The early Christians impressed the culture with *high moral standards* and their practice of *charity for all, regardless of social status*" (emphasis added). Today's church could earn a doctorate in cultural impact just by integrating those two qualities into the fabric of daily life.

Philosopher and writer Justin was first drawn to Christianity because of the supernatural courage and dignity of believers martyred for their faith. His conversion from well-schooled philosopher to believer in Christ is a classic evangelistic example for the church today. Justin was a seeker of truth. His studies led him from Stoicism to Pythagoreanism to Platoism. The courage of the

Christian martyrs sparked an initial interest. He wrote that a chance meeting (I'd call it a divine appointment) with an aged Christian man in Ephesus led to his conversion. "Straightaway a flame was kindled in my soul," Justin wrote, "and a love of the prophets and those who are friends of Christ possessed me." Justin realized that every philosophy has a portion of truth, and he wrote that Platoism served as "a schoolmaster to bring us to Christ."

One of Justin's interesting observations is contained in *The Second Apology.* He argued that Christians make good citizens. He wrote that it is a misunderstanding to think that followers of Christ undermine the foundation of society. Sound familiar? Today he would be writing to the ACLU. It seems that the nature of man remains the same, just repackaged in modern wrappings.

Christ's teachings on the dignity of life greatly influenced the early church. Remember that the early Christians lived in a pagan culture that practiced infanticide, gladiator combat, and even cannibalism. The church's revolutionary view of the value of life was sacrificially demonstrated during the two great plagues that devastated the empire in the second and third centuries. While pagans avoided any contact with the sick and even cast them into the streets while still alive, Christians nursed and cared for the sick even though it cost some their lives. The selfless service of the early church won many Gentile converts to the fold.

One other element of the early church explosion is worth noting. Those who showed interest in the faith were not immediately given full responsibility in the fold. They were first given instruction in the faith, according to the writer Hippolytus. Then a discipleship process lasting from three to six years helped the new believer develop a genuine and firm commitment. I wonder if today we don't tend to rush new believers into positions of service and responsibility before they are fully grounded in their relationship with Christ. I have seen new Christians become elders or church board members in a matter of months. Maybe I am just a slow learner, but I would not have been ready to serve in such a capacity that soon in my Christian experience. But I am not sure in retrospect that I wouldn't have thought I was ready.

WHAT THE CHURCH HAS DONE (AND CONTINUES TO DO) RIGHT

Throughout history the church has been most effective when serving. Winifred Kirkland said the best "argument for the risen Christ is the living Christian." And the best argument of the living Christian is one that is serving. We have much to learn about service from the example of the early church.

In fact, throughout history, revival in the church seems to initiate service, or service initiates revival. Whether chicken or egg, the two seem to go hand in hand. Great men and women of faith have had a lasting and profound effect on history. John Wesley gathered over 350,000 signatures on a petition to end slave trade. I am not sure if we could generate those kinds of numbers today on similarly significant issues. Think about that. Today I heard a radio ministry appealing for support of a petition to ban partial birth abortions. They were hoping for three hundred thousand names with the help of radio and the Internet. I realized then the miracle of Wesley's faith and commitment.

Bishop William Wilberforce is widely credited with helping to end slave ownership. He was referred to by Madame de Stael as the "wittiest man in England and the most religious" (a combo many would think impossible). He grew up hearing the preaching of an ex-slave trader and slave-ship captain named John Newton. Reverend Newton's salvation experience and resulting call to ministry ultimately prompted him to write the hymn "Amazing Grace." When Newton talked about the grace that could "save a wretch like me," it was more than just a lyric; he had lived it.

But Wilberforce fell away from the faith and spent several years as a Member of Parliament and general party guy ("the temptations of the table," as he called it). He recommitted his life to faith in Christ and, in 1787, set out by God's grace to effect the "suppression of the slave trade and reformation of morals." You probably know the rest. Wilberforce was a major force in the ultimate abolition of the slave trade. His thoughts on the cultural responsibilities of a Christian are sobering for me. "A man who acts from the principles I profess," he wrote, "reflects that he is to give an account of his political conduct at the judgment seat of Christ."

Wow. That is a succinct and convicting statement of the responsibility that believers take on when we profess the principles of Christ. There is no condemnation in failure, but there is an obligation of devotion to our Lord. I can do better. We can do better. We must do more for the principles and the name of Christ that we profess. One man or woman can make a difference. As Pascal observed, "The entire sea is altered by a single stone."

Anthony Ashley Cooper (who would later be known as Lord Ashley and Lord Shaftesbury) began his British Parliamentary career in 1826. A devout Christian, he crusaded for child labor laws to abolish the horrible working conditions common for children. He also established the ten-hour workday for factory workers (that was considered progress then). He worked to provide care for the mentally ill. He was a classic example of how to combine the dual citizenship of heaven and earth that we discussed in chapter 10.

Lord Ashley commented on his life of social reform by saying, "My religious views are not very popular, but they are the views that have sustained and comforted me all through my life. I think a man's religion, if it is worth anything, should enter into every sphere of life, and rule his conduct in every relation. I have always been—and, please God, always shall be—an Evangelical."

Amen. Ashley is an example of a man who had a clearly defined worldview characterized by faith in Christ, and that worldview was ingrained enough to permeate his every action.

What is often neglected when Christianity is discussed is the incredible number and reach of charitable organizations started by followers of Jesus Christ. Thousands upon thousands of Christians took seriously the commandment to love their neighbors.

For example, the Salvation Army provides a staggering amount of services through six thousand facilities in the United States, and it offers worldwide relief in over on hundred countries. The YMCA provides programs and facilities for over fourteen million people. (As I write these words on March 1, I am reminded and grateful that a YMCA instructor came up with a little indoor game to pass the time in the winter. We owe March Madness and the American sport of basketball to James Naismith and the YMCA.) And Goodwill Industries was providing employment for the disabled and poor before we could even spell "politically correct," and it is still the nation's largest nonprofit provider of employment training for those groups. International relief organizations like World Vision, Catholic Relief Services, Feed the Children,

Christian Children's Fund, Compassion International, and Food for the Poor provide food, medicine, and other essential services around the world. A list of inner-city ministries, camps for the disadvantaged, homes for troubled youth, and other outreaches would double the size of this book.

The number of opportunities available to Christians who want to serve is mind-boggling. What would be the impact if every evangelical believer committed to a personal outreach just once a month?

God of course continues to call men and women to great works for Him today. Millard and Linda Fuller became millionaires before age thirty. But restlessness in their souls led them to recommit to their faith. The Fullers subsequently sold all their possessions, gave the money to the poor, and began looking for a new direction. The direction that God took them was to found a little ministry called Habitat for Humanity. Today more than one hundred thousand families have safe, affordable housing in more than sixty countries around the world. Over half a million people have a home because one couple was willing to see what God could do through them if they totally trusted Him.

SPECTATOR OR PARTICIPANT?

I look with awe and humility at what the Fullers did. Could I do what they did? More to the point, *would* I do what they did? When I look at men and women who have accomplished great things for Christ, I tend to feel like the characters from the movie *Wayne's World* who bowed down before a rock icon and repeated, "We're not worthy. We're not worthy." What the Fullers did scares me, to be honest. I fear that if I really sell out to God, He'll ask me to do what the Fullers did. That is an area of personal growth and faith that I am seeking to improve.

So what keeps me from giving more? The sin of busyness comes to mind. It is hard (though tempting) to deny that selfishness is a factor. Busyness, selfishness, and nearly every other "ness" that we can offer is likely rooted in pride. C. S. Lewis observed that "pride leads to every other vice: it is the complete anti-God state of mind." The first time I read that statement, it struck me as so bold that my American mind-set immediately objected. But I have yet to meet a sin or vice whose roots cannot be traced back to pride. Pride is not content with having money. Pride wants more than the neighbor or coworker. Pride is not satisfied with having a serviceable and dependable car. Pride wants the best and newest and best equipped. Pride keeps me from giving more because my needs trump those of a suffering and needy world. I am not thrilled to be writing these words because I am guilty as charged. But it is true. And I reflect back on the words of Wilberforce (and I paraphrase), "A person who acts from the principles he professes must give an account at the judgment seat of Christ." We don't like to think much about that, do we? Our salvation is not at stake, and so we would prefer to treat our actions on earth like a speeding ticket. Delayed adjudication is more comfortable than facing the truth now.

More on pride. Pride does not rest on having a mate who has been faithful and loving. No, pride wants a trophy spouse who is more attractive than the wives of your buddies. It is pride that says you deserve better. I deserve to be happy, don't I? That is the mantra of the selfish. Think about the arrogance of that. Did you deserve to be born in the most prosperous nation in history? Did you deserve to be gifted with the skills to make more money in a week than entire families in other countries make in a year? If you opted for the trophy mate, did your kids deserve to be from a broken home? Did your spouse deserve to be left behind because he or she is not as attractive as the person you can now attract?

It was pride that led to the downfall of Adam and Eve in the garden. It was pride that caused Satan himself to try to overthrow God and be like God. It was pride that led to the first murder (Genesis 4) and pride that led to King David's downfall. Pride even affected the disciples. Twelve men who were mentored by Christ Himself drew his ire by bickering over which one would be greatest in heaven (Mark 9:34). We look at that and wonder, "How could they be so stupid? How could anyone be so stupid?"

Then my nemesis (the mirror) reflects a man who can be (and often is) that stupid.

Some might think I have a negative attitude about life. I prefer to think that it is candid and realistic, but I realize my views on sin are not likely to featured on *Oprah:* "Oprah, I am a wretched sinner. Can I have a hug?"

The simple little three-letter word *sin* makes us either squirm or mock the concept. In *The Other Side,* John Alexander wrote, "Sin is the best news there is...because with sin there's a way out. You can't repent of confusion or psychological flaws inflicted by your parents—you're stuck with them. But you can repent of sin. Sin and repentance are the only grounds for hope and joy, the grounds for reconciled, joyful relationships." Understanding sin is understanding the why of human behavior. G. K. Chesterton felt that original sin or the sin nature of man was "the only religious doctrine that can be scientifically, empirically verified. All you have to do is observe people."

For over forty years I have dealt with frustration about my distractibility and lack of concentration. My disorganization has been a constant struggle. When I read about research into Attention Deficit Disorder, I was relieved. I was not the only person in the world who struggled with this. When I recognized what it was, I could deal with it. Now my reaction is not "What's wrong with me?" Instead, I know that this is how I'm wired and can allow for how I act and react as I seek to accomplish whatever task is at hand.

Along the same lines, understanding the concept of sin actually became liberating for my faith. I had figured out awhile back that I wasn't always good. (I have an amazing gift of self-awareness.) I knew that my motives weren't always right (see?). And that pride was an enemy. Realizing that all humans are born that way helps me to quit struggling and start dealing with it. Dealing with it means you and I repent, pray, and depend daily on the Holy Spirit.

But we live in a world of microwave oatmeal because we can't wait five minutes to cook it on the stove. We now have instant credit in order to buy all those unneeded things without the annoying requirement of actual money. The exercise equipment infomercials concentrate on how little time you can spare to get in shape. I flip from wretched cable station to wretched cable station trying to find the workout machine that will make me look and feel great in one minute per day. We tend to view the prospects of growing in our faith in the same way. How easily can I get off and still be highly thought of by other Christians?

Being a follower of Christ means running counter to the culture. Spiritual maturity is not instant. Loving your neighbor is not easy. Having an impact on the culture is not a hobby activity for weekends. Faith that is real is lived out in everyday life. I wish I could rationalize that away. But spiritual renewal will come only when we consistently engage others with a faith that matters. That means touching and going out among them as well as pledging and tithing. Timothy wrote, "The Lord knows those who are his," and, "Everyone who confesses the name of the Lord must turn away from wickedness" (2 Timothy 2:19).

A political pundit once said that being a conscience is not the same thing as having one. It is not my desire to be a critical conscience for you while ignoring my own sin and pride. There is an African proverb that says the best time to plant a tree is twenty years ago. The next best time is today.

If you started planting the tree of spiritual growth and maturity twenty years ago, then praise God and keep the roots growing deep. For the rest of us, whaddya say we start planting today?

Chapter 16

Loose Ends

A couple walks into the dentist's office and the husband is
obviously in a hurry to get the procedure over with.

"Doc," he says, "nothing fancy. No needles, no gas. Let's pull
this tooth and get it done quick."

The dentist is surprised by the man's stoic approach. "I'm
impressed. I wish all of my patients had your courage. Now
which tooth is it?"

The husband turned to his wife and said, "Show him your
tooth, honey."

—http://www.emazing.com JOKE OF THE DAY

I pray that I have not come across in this book like the man at the
dentist's office, blithely suggesting painful remedies for everyone
while I comfortably observe from the waiting room. It is always
easier to recommend corrective actions for other people. I hope
that I have made it very clear that I am also challenging myself to
step it up a level for Christ. I realize that I have ruffled some feath-
ers, but remember that my desire was to get you out of your comfort bunker. I hope I have given you some things to think about.

I am very good at identifying problems, although I admit that is not a skill that is in short supply. I have been very candid about problems in our Christian family. Rebecca Manley Pippert talked about the Christian journey in *Servant* magazine: "God is making us holy. But there is a requirement for learning how to submit to God's authority: humility. We won't get very far in the development of holiness if we are defensive about our flaws. That is why holy people are so easy to be with. They have been around God too long to try to pretend they are perfect. They are the first to acknowledge their pride and their faults."

Let me hasten to say that I have not yet arrived in the category she describes. But that is the destination I'm after.

We Christians have a wonderful opportunity to impact our culture. George Barna found that half of all unchurched and non-Christian adults admit that they are seeking meaning and purpose. "These people are not dumb," Barna's report stated, "but they don't put much time or thought into developing an internally consistent religious belief system. The result is that a lot of what they say they believe doesn't fit together very well."

That is why I think it is so important for Christians to be prepared to address the doubts, questions, and criticisms of seekers. We must understand what the gospel is and how to communicate it effectively. We must demonstrate love and an attitude of service to others. And we must grow in Christ and offer something different from what society offers.

Over the course of my life, I have encountered all types of people who claimed the title *Christian*. Some tended to drive me away from the faith. The belief system they possessed clearly wasn't working, and I didn't need something else that didn't work. But I was fortunate to meet and observe several people who demonstrated something truly different in their lives. These Christians lived a kind of life that drew my interest and ultimately led to my embracing of the faith.

In the movie *Field of Dreams,* the character played by Kevin Costner keeps getting a vision about building a baseball field. Costner hears a voice say, "If you build it, they will come." There is a quiet voice speaking to us that simply says, "If you live it, they will hear. They will see. And they will come."

Acerbic columnist Herb Caen observed, "The trouble with born-again Christians is that they are a bigger pain the second time around." We must admit that sometimes he is right. God forgive us for being an unnecessary pain to others. I believe in the ultimate judgment of God, but there is so much more that is relevant about the Christian faith to seekers. Christianity is a faith that answers every important question we face—and we have done a poor job of modeling that faith.

A discussion of faith should never involve badgering. Forced conversions that don't last tend to alienate those victims (I use the word advisedly) for years or even forever. I know that many people resent the fact that Christians "feel compelled to proselytize." The P word has become a scathing indictment of evangelicals in our pluralistic world. So what are Christians to do? Can we fail to do what we believe God has called us to do? Can we quench our desire to tell about the most important thing in our lives?

I would propose this Bill of Rights for Unbelievers:
- I have the right to never have faith forced on me.
- I have the right to never be treated in a condescending manner.

- I have the right to always hear the truth.
- I have the right for you to patiently hear my concerns and doubts.
- I have the right to seek answers to those questions and doubts that you can't answer.
- I have the right to be steered to resources for my own study and investigation.
- I have the right to be loved no matter how I respond to the gospel message.

We certainly must continue to lovingly express our faith to those around us. But we also owe them the opportunity to allow God to finish His work in them.

THE REST OF THE STORY

Earlier I promised to tell you the rest of the story about our daughter, Katie. When she was born the doctors did not expect her to live more than a few hours. We were blessed to have a one-year birthday party for Katie despite those early opinions.

When our daughter was three months old, Joni decided she would like to have another baby. I wasn't sure. What if the birth defect manifested itself again? I lacked the faith in God's mercy and provision that Joni demonstrated. Even so, we did decide to trust God, and Joni became pregnant again.

Just thirteen months after Katie joined us, a perfectly healthy baby boy named Brett joined the family. Life was really crazy with my travel schedule, Katie, and now three sons aged eight, five and brand-new. In May 1986, Joni and I made plans to get away for an evening. We had a nurse come stay with Katie and also look after

Brett, and we dropped off the older boys at a friend's house so Joni and I could go to the theatre. Returning home after picking up the boys at the sitter, we pulled into the garage and started to get out of the car. Suddenly two men with black masks burst into our garage shouting at us not to move. Both had guns. It was the most surreal and terrifying single moment of my life. What could I do? There were two of them, and I would have had to be Jackie Chan to take them on. Even if I was, could I risk a member of my family being shot?

They herded us into the house. One of the gunmen held the boys, Joni, and the nurse at gunpoint. The leader walked me around the house and threatened my family if I didn't reveal where things were stashed. Joni prayed fervently in the living room. I had a supernatural calm (believe me, it was not of my own doing) that allowed me to engage the robber in conversation. He asked for all of our cash. I had none. Then he got angry at me because we didn't have more cash in the house. I actually was yelling back at him, saying our daughter was going to die and all of our money had gone to medical bills. I guess the frustration of Katie's situation plus his rude demeanor set me off. Joni was convinced I would be shot, but we learned later that this duo was more aggressive when the husband acted timidly. Our oldest son, Matt, heard the exchange and offered what he could. "Mr. Robber," he said, "you can have my piggy bank." They actually took it.

All the while, Katie slept quietly in her room. Both intruders were freaked out by Katie. I guess they thought she had something contagious since she was going to die and a nurse was in the house. They steered a wide path around her room. When they left, the robbers forced us into a bedroom and jammed the door shut from the outside. The bedroom these rocket scientists locked us into had a common bathroom with Katie's room. As soon as they left, I was able to go through her room and outside to my car phone (they had cut our phone lines) to call the police.

I will always be convinced that Katie stayed with us for two reasons. For one, God preserved her life until after Brett joined us. Second, I believe she stayed to be our protective guardian angel during that robbery. Those guys did much worse things in other robberies before they were caught. We felt blessed to have lost only material things. All that mattered was still safe. You can disagree with me about Katie's purpose in living fourteen months past her predicted life span. I don't care. All the medical opinions were that she would only live a few days. In my heart, there was a reason.

Just a few weeks after the robbery, Katie's heart began to fail. On June 15, 1986, Katie died. Remember the earlier story about the family photo? Katie could not smile. Her only facial expression was a sort of frown or grimace. But when Katie's life began to ebb away, there was a feeling of peace in the room. As her spirit left her—and for the first time in her short life—Katie had a big smile. I will always believe that she was responding to a heavenly escort.

At her memorial service we had an unusual request for a song to honor our daughter. One of the songs we picked was made famous by singer Bette Midler, not the type of artist you would normally think of for a memorial service. The song was entitled *The Rose,* and the lyrics just seemed to fit our little girl.

> When the night has been too lonely,
> And the road has been too long
> And you think that love is only

For the lucky and the strong
Just remember in the winter
Far beneath the bitter snows
Lies the seed, that with the sun's love,
In the spring becomes the rose.

For Joni and me, Katie's precious soul was the seed, her birth defect the bitter snow. When she died, the Son's love came and turned our daughter into a rose.

Unlike the church that initially rejected Katie and us, many Christians demonstrated Jesus' love over the course of Katie's life. Joni was blessed with a babysitting co-op of Christian women who not only accepted Katie but asked for opportunities to care for her. That love and acceptance from these Christian women was vital to our healing. In an earlier chapter I mentioned the pastor who welcomed our family. Joni was sustained by the wonderful women in her Bible Study Fellowship group. Without these obedient Christians, who knows what detours Joni and I might have taken on our spiritual journey?

So that is the rest of Katie's story. As for me, I want to live the kind of life that will make Katie proud until we meet. I heard a wonderful testimony from a Christian woman here in Dallas. Alvanetta was the wife of a local high-school football coach named James Jones who died last summer. Sympathizers told Alvanetta that they were sorry she had lost James. She smiled, looked at them, and said, "I didn't lose him. I know exactly where he is." That is what I want my wife and sons to say when my time is up: "We didn't lose him. We know exactly where he is. He is getting to know his little girl."

Chapter 17

Now What?

If we take care of the inches, we will not have to worry about the miles.

—HARLEY COLERIDGE

We have covered a lot of territory over the past sixteen chapters. If you have felt a bit uncomfortable here and there, then welcome to the club. With any Christian book, you face a basic question at the end: Now what? I have purposely not led you through chapter-by-chapter exercises and fill-in-the-blank quizzes. But I do think it is important that each of us identifies at least a couple of areas where God might be speaking to us.

There are two questions I think we should prayerfully ask ourselves every single day:

- Today, have I represented my title "Christian" in a way that glorifies Jesus?
- If I have not, how can I repair the damage and/or do better tomorrow?

It is an important and sacred responsibility to claim to be a follower of Christ. Many of us take our identification with a college, club, or cause more seriously than our faith in terms of how it actually affects our daily lives. That should never be! We must—both individually and corporately—take more seriously our responsibilities as representatives of Christ.

To follow is a list of some of things I discussed in this book. I would ask you to honestly evaluate, on a scale of 1 to 10, your need to improve on these issues. In our scale, 1 means you are doing all right for a sinner, 5 means you could use a tune-up, and 10 is a spiritual 911. You need help and you need it quick. Be honest. This is between you and God.

_____ I need to be more friendly to the people I don't know in my church.

_____ I need to develop more friendships with unchurched people.

_____ I need to evaluate my priorities in light of the question, "Would Jesus spend His time on this?"

_____ I need to quit using Christian "language" with the unchurched and learn how to explain spiritual terms in language they'll understand.

_____ I have racial issues that I must confess and give to God for healing.

_____ I need to give more of my financial resources to God's work.

_____ I need to give more of my time to God's work.

_____ I need to better understand and be able to explain my Christian worldview.

_____ I need to learn more about the teachings of Jesus.

_____ I need to understand what I believe and be able to articulate those beliefs to others.

_____ I need my Christian walk to more closely match my Christian talk.

_____ I need to ask forgiveness and repair damage I have done to other Christians.

Take a look at those issues that need the most improvement. Give them the highest priority. Pick one today and start asking God to help you improve in that area. Being a Christian is not about works. Nonetheless, to be more effective in our faith we must show up each day with an attitude of "How can I serve Christ better today?" There will certainly be moments, even days and weeks, when we will be "bad Christians." But that is not where God wants us to be, and I would guess that is not where you want to be either. When we lean on the power of prayer, the Holy Spirit, God's Word, the joy of grace, and the daily realization that we are His representatives every time we walk out the door, we can, and we must, do better. In the words of Mother Teresa, "We can do no great things, only small things with great love." Let's determine to be "good" Christians, not in order to earn Brownie points, but solely to glorify our Lord. Join me in giving God the inches of love. We can trust Him for the miles.

If you would like
to contact Dave Burchett,
please visit his Web site at
http://www.daveburchett.com.